With an infinitely readable style, Mary's marketing advice cuts to the chase. *Word of Mouth, Mouse, and Mobile* is a great follow-up to her first book, *Five-Minute Marketing.*
—Jeff Korhan, New Media and Small Business Marketing Expert, bestselling author of *Built in Social: Essential Social Marketing Practices for Every Small Business*

Today positive word of mouth may be the single greatest influencer of a brand's future success. If you want to know how to succeed Mary's book is a great place to start.
—Lance Saunders, Executive VP, Managing Director, DDB Canada

The marketing how-to advice continues in *Word of Mouth, Mouse, and Mobile.* This is a great sequel to *Five-Minute Marketing* for those who enjoy Mary's crisp, quick-read style.
—Laura McBride, Director Client Services, Station X

As a marketing expert and exceptional instructor, Mary offers a rare combination of academic and practical experience.
—Teresita Ireneo-Manalo, Ph.D., Dean, Acsenda School of Management, Vancouver

Mary sees the world through a set of different eyes, and has the creativity to make connections that are not obvious, make sense. When applied to marketing, it's brilliant.
—Suzan Beattie, B.A., LL.B., Canadian Association of Professional Speakers, Vancouver Chapter Chair

Mary is a marketing expert with great insights and a sharp eye for innovative and effective marketing strategies.
—Laine McDonald, Education Services Manager, Small Business BC

Engaging, entertaining, and a born teacher, Mary makes learning fun. From the classroom to the boardroom, she offers up great marketing insights. This book is simply an extension of her style to the written page.
—Charlene Hill, Department Chair, School of Business, Capilano University

T0367645

word of
MOUTH
MOUSE &
MOBILE

*A sequel to 5minutemarketing with more quick-read
insights to leverage your story in an accelerated world.*

Mary Charleson, MBA

www.charleson.ca
www.fiveminutemarketing.com

Order this book online at www.trafford.com
or email orders@trafford.com

Most Trafford titles are also available at major online book retailers.

Printed in the United States of America.

ISBN: 978-1-4907-0587-3 (sc)
ISBN: 978-1-4907-0588-0 (hc)
ISBN: 978-1-4907-0611-5 (e)

Library of Congress Control Number: 2013911083

Trafford rev. 07/08/2013

 www.trafford.com

North America & international
toll-free: 1 888 232 4444 (USA & Canada)
fax: 812 355 4082

For Nancy, my lifelong guide and mentor
For Chris, my source of encouragement
And for Alex and Pat, my inspiration

Contents

Acknowledgements

. . .

I am a marketer and I love speaking, writing, and consulting. It is with pride that I can say I've pursued my passion and have achieved success for over twenty years in the private sector with my own consulting company, Charleson Communications. There are many who have helped me realize this accomplishment. Thanks to Doug Argue and Sharman King, two successful Vancouver entrepreneurs, now retired, who gave me those first consulting contracts way back, which allowed me to launch my business. Thanks to the hundreds of clients along the way that put trust in me to advise them. Thanks to Elaine Allison, Stephen Hammond, and Cheryl Cran, three respected international speakers who introduced me to the Canadian Association of Professional Speakers and helped me realize my potential in this industry. Thanks to Ian Noble, who gave me my first column in *Business in Vancouver* back in 2002, and to Tim Renshaw, my current editor. Thanks to Teresita Ireneo-Manalo who first saw my potential as a teacher at City University of Seattle. Thanks to Victor Crapnell for the fabulous cover design for this book. Victor, you are truly a pleasure to work with! And finally I'd like to thank my family—my husband Chris and my children, Alex and Pat, who engage my daily observations and discussions on marketing, and Nancy Holborn, my mom, mentor, and inspiration.

Introduction

. . .

I have always enjoyed writing as a creative venue and a platform to share with others. It has been a distinct pleasure to be a marketing columnist for *Business in Vancouver* for now well over ten years. During that time, I have also been honoured to have work published in national publications, such as *Marketing Magazine*, *Strategy*, *Zoomer* magazine, *Cottage* magazine, and the *Toronto Star*. Frankly when I first received an editorial planner for the year as a new marketing columnist, I questioned whether I would have enough ideas to make it through. But what I quickly learned was there were endless angles to be explored, emerging technologies that were changing the face of marketing, and a plethora of great business examples that others could learn from.

My first book, *Five-Minute Marketing*, was born from the content of my previously published work. It helped launch my speaking career as well as my www.fiveminutemarketing.com blog, which became another platform to share short editorial pieces that could be read in five minutes or less. My goal with speaking and writing was to help a growing roster of entrepreneurs, business owners, marketing managers, and students, who were my clients, learn about marketing. My second book, *Word of Mouth, Mouse, and Mobile*, is a continuation of the same theme. It is a sequel to *Five-Minute Marketing* with even more quick-read insights to leverage your story in an accelerated world. While some pieces have been published previously, many have not. They needed to be shared with a broader audience.

In addition to speaking, writing, and consulting for companies throughout Canada and the US, I have enjoyed leading entrepreneur marketing sessions for Small Business BC, which, while delivered in person to a Vancouver-based audience, are often telecast throughout British Columbia, Alberta, and Saskatchewan. I have also had the pleasure of being sought to teach marketing at several US and Canadian universities, including New York Institute of Technology, City University of Seattle, Acsenda School of Management Vancouver, University Canada West, and Capilano University.

The irony of having been raised in a long line of university professors and teachers has not been lost on me as I have ventured, initially somewhat reluctantly, into the teaching realm. While I consider speaking, writing, and running a successful marketing consulting business the pinnacle of my career accomplishments, it was only on becoming a teacher that my mom felt that I had truly arrived. They say we never really stop striving to seek the approval of our mothers, but I have to honestly say, Nancy, that I don't think of what I do as teaching. I simply share knowledge and ideas, and inspire others to learn.

That then is at the core of this book—a desire to inspire others to learn through sharing stories with marketing insight that can be read quickly and put to work in your business.

The title, *Word of Mouth, Mouse, and Mobile*, was born from a phrase I often use when doing presentations and keynotes. Increasingly we live in a world where we are all connected, and those connections, both online and off, are pivotal in the sharing of stories, gaining publicity, and garnering a following for our businesses, products, or services. So please enjoy. Dip in or read it cover to cover, and ramp up your marketing quickly.

If you like what you see here, why not sign up for my regular blog post alerts here: www.fiveminutemarketing.com/subscribe/ And if you'd like to get marketing tips delivered directly to your in box, subscribe to my marketing e-newsletter. Visit www.charleson.ca and select 'Join our mailing list' on the home page.

word of

M UTH
M USE &
M BILE

CHAPTER 1

Generating WOM, Publicity and Leveraging Social Media

. . .

We are all connected. Never before in history has this statement been so true. Whether it's online or off, the platforms to share stories are readily available to leverage your business. This fact was driven home to me recently when, with the assistance of Facebook, mobile phones, and friendship, I was able to locate and have my lost luggage returned. You can read all about this crazy tale in the chapter-opening article. I use this signature story in my presentations to not only demonstrate the incredible power of word of mouth, mouse, and mobile, but to also demonstrate how I have leveraged the story for business publicity. Leveraging social media and publicity is the theme for the first chapter. I hope you'll be inspired with some ideas for your own business!

How Facebook Found My Luggage and a Lesson on How We Are All Connected

. . .

I was recently travelling on business and had the occasion to be transferring planes in Toronto on Friday, February 8, 2013. That's the day that Ontario and the whole east coast were hammered by one of the worst snowstorms in decades. Arriving from snowless Vancouver en route to Montreal, I knew immediately that my connecting flight would not be taking off anytime soon. I based this intuitive grasp of the obvious on the sight of the 401, normally a 16-lane freeway that appeared as a single lane, two-track path, without a vehicle in sight.

Most flights in and out of Toronto were not going anywhere anytime soon. Looking like it had been pulled from the screen of *Planes, Trains and Automobiles*, the departures board listing 'cancelled' beside most flights didn't look promising. Twelve hours and numerous delayed, cancelled, and rebooked flights later, I was on my way to Montreal. While I always travel with a carry-on for business, I had checked a bag of gear for a day skating on the Ottawa canal with a friend during the return leg home Monday. I had tagged it well and secured the handles together, a key factor, as you'll see later. Of course no Air Canada flight experience is complete without a delayed flight and lost luggage, and on both counts, the airline delivered. With no bag in sight in Montreal, I filed forms, got my reference number, and headed to the hotel, now twenty-four hours since departing Vancouver.

But that's when the story deviates from the usual lost bag tale. The following day, a friend departed Vancouver bound for Toronto also with Air Canada. While we learned of her time imposition on Facebook with flight delays, it was the photo that she posted that caught my eye later that evening. She had taken a picture of hundreds of bags pulled from the carousel in Toronto without an owner in sight. While I was out having dinner, prior to seeing the post, a lengthy discussion had broken out on her wall musing whether one of the bags could possibly be mine. I picked up the thread later that evening and was quite amazed to see what was most certainly my bag—the blue one, now marked in the photo, with the handles tied together—remember?

Photo: Mary Charleson

What makes this story so memorable to this point is the fact that prior to having gone out for dinner, I had logged into Air Canada missing luggage site and had been greeted with the message that my claim had 'no matching record', meaning the name and claim number did not match and the bag did not exist. To now see my lost bag in Toronto airport via Facebook was quite something!

Of course my initial euphoric call to Air Canada to share my news was met with a guarded response. Just how many bags get claimed via a Facebook photo ID? But I decided to call back an hour later and re-frame the story, stating, 'I have managed to track my lost bag in a rather unconventional way, and I would like to *make you the hero* of my story.' Simply by adding a personal touch and involving this person in the tale, they became engaged and wanted to help. They promised to see what could be done.

When I arrived at Montreal airport the following day to catch my flight to Ottawa, I checked on my bag status. It still officially had 'no matching record', however my ticket name reference had a field note that said a bag had been put on a Toronto-Montreal flight and should arrive in time for my connection to Ottawa. Clearly the hero of my story had something to do with this!

While the bag missed that flight too, it did eventually reunite with me in Ottawa. And I can say with certainty that although it did have a name and address attached to it, it's quite likely it would have been days before that bag would have seen Vancouver if not for Facebook and my friend's photo.

The technology of smartphones and Facebook certainly facilitated the exercise. But in the end, it was the power of storytelling and involving others in the message that helped spread the word. I think there's a powerful marketing message there. While we should certainly keep up with technology and utilise the latest tools, they in themselves are not marketing. It is the human touch and storytelling that should be at the heart of your message.

And yes, despite the routine customer service issues that seem rife at Air Canada, there is a hero there with a story to tell!

I have since been able to leverage this story into coverage by Global TV, articles on customer service, and speaking engagements on the power of social media. One simple random event and a connected world yielded a huge publicity opportunity. What story could you leverage for business gain using word of mouth, mouse, and mobile?

7 Tips for Creating Content That Begs To Be Shared on Social Media

■ ■ ■

We likely all remember the classic scene from *Lady and the Tramp* where two dogs slurp up spaghetti, only to realize upon their snouts meeting that they were eating the same piece. It's an iconic image of love and sharing. Wouldn't it be great if, in leveraging your influence, you could evoke that same urge to share your content by your followers?

But the first thing to consider is the reason *why* people share your stuff. Here's a big hint: It's not about you, it's about *them*! In my experience, people share content that makes them:

- Look smart
- Look connected
- Look funny
- Look insightful

If you can provide content that allows your readers to appear smart, connected, funny, or insightful, the chances of it getting shared go up exponentially. While this is a subtle shift of thinking, it makes sense.

The key to writing great content is to not only have valuable information, but to have something that lends itself to a great headline that people will want to open, link to, and ultimately share. Here are some ideas:

1. **Lists.** In an abbreviated world of sound-bite communication, lists will resonate. (Example: 10 ways to improve your blog.)

2. **How to do something.** The world loves a teacher especially if there is a willing pupil. (Example: 5 sure-fire ways to get publicity.)

3. **Facts and statistics.** Generally statistics only get people excited if they are proving something unexpected. Graphic presentations work best. (Example: Facebook and Twitter user statistics just released.)

4. **Negative spin.** Zig when others zag. In a world of 'how to' advice, 'how not to' can cut through the clutter. (Example: 5 reasons people are not reading your Tweets.)

5. **Research.** Quote research from respected sources and all parties instantly appear smarter! (Example: Yale studies on why women CEOs fail.)

6. **Case study.** Nothing gets better than real-life application when it comes to learning. (Example: Social media disasters of 2012.)

7. **News story.** Put your own spin on a news story, or if you can, break news yourself. I did this recently when news broke that Sam Sung was working for Apple in Vancouver. Since I live there, I was able to add my own spin to the story by doing my own journalistic investigation (http://fiveminutemarketing.com/2012/11/sam-sung-a-specialist-for-apple/). (Example: Does Sam Sung really work for Apple?)

And if you're curious about that last story, and the subsequent follow-up, it does appear later in this book, so do keep reading!

What's Your Summertime Blue Ocean Strategy?

• • •

While casting about on the beautiful Pacific Northwest waters of the Sunshine Coast recently, I found myself reflecting on my personal 'blue ocean strategy'. In marketing terms, a blue ocean strategy is when a business pursues a new product or new market, essentially playing in open water with few competitors, while others battle it out in the 'red ocean' where competitive sharks are fighting for an already-defined and mature market segment.

Beyond the immediate and obvious observation that indeed I was by myself, paddling on a peaceful stretch of glistening early morning water, I realized that while as a marketing consultant and educator, I was quick to give advice to others, perhaps it was time to take some of my own advice. What was my personal blue ocean strategy for positioning my business? It is usually only in those times of reflection away from work that we are able to see the big picture and focus our efforts for when we return. I think that's why I love our cottage escape up the coast so much. I can relax and step back, but also think and strategize.

I've been on Google+ for some time now. I am there largely because of the ability it seems to have to drive search results. That, and I've found some really interesting and intelligent people in my fields of interest that deliver information I couldn't find elsewhere. And I've been able to connect with them globally. While it initially seemed largely a playground of techie guys, I have started to notice a few signs that make me think this is a blue ocean worth swimming in more. Perhaps it's a bit of a backlash against Facebook and their Machiavellian approach to maximize market value for shareholders, while using their members and their associated profiles and connections, as pawns in their game. Or maybe it's just some very unscientific anecdotal observations within my circle of contacts, but I have definitely experienced a growth in requests for both Google+ and LinkedIn lately. While I actively use Facebook for friends, and pursue the growth of my Facebook business page (www.facebook.com/fiveminutemarketing), until recently Facebook content was not maximized for search. My Google+ content is. Google also recently linked up a 'Local' button on G+ profiles that further pushes search results within a defined geographic area, tagged by search term categories of your own choosing. This teamed up with the growth of the mobile web, smartphones, and tablets makes it easy to see that being on Google+ is going to be a necessity for most small businesses. Interactivity for customer reviews is all built in, and YouTube videos that you may choose to link also become part of your profile.

I intend to actively build my presence on Google+ where the ocean is blue and inviting for business. I invite you take your business for a swim with me and establish yourself as a big fish before the millions of minnows join us.

The Machiavellian Mad Men Have Left the Building

. . .

For years Madison Avenue advertising executives considered consumers as targets. Watch one episode of *Mad Men*, and there can be little doubt as to the arrogant Machiavellian approach of that time to marketing. Although we've come a long way since the 1960s, marketers rolled through the '70s, '80s, and '90s seemingly unaware that there could ever be anyone in control of the message other than them. To this day, marketing students are still taught about marketing and segmentation as though it was something that could be precisely found and influenced.

But in the new world order of the internet and social media, consumers are no longer the prey. They are the predators. The roll of control has shifted. In many cases, schools and business leaders are struggling to catch up. How should we now redefine the way we teach marketing? More importantly, how do we advise our clients or implement changes in our own business to respond to this new reality?

In the new marketplace, 'a company or brand is not what it says it is, but *what it does*.' These wise words, spoken by Bruce Philp, keynote speaker at the recent BCAMA Vision Marketing Conference, are on the mark for today's consumer reality. I bought a copy of his book, *Consumer Republic*, at the conference. It is the first time I've read a marketing book that has allowed me to reconcile the oft-conflicting personal interests of marketing and consumerism for business gain and a deeply held, left-leaning value of the need for social justice in society.

Ultimately Philp believes that branded consumerism is about empowerment. He makes a pretty compelling case that consumers throughout time have been in control of brands, and that by having the ability to influence others online through social media today, we are simply returning to the way it always was throughout history. He thinks the heady days of the last thirty years featuring command and control precision targeting of the advertising world were simply an aberration where business falsely came to believe they held the power. He just might be right.

The marketplace today is a forum. Into that forum, we place our brands. But rather than running a limited time advertising campaign to position a produce or boost sales, we are actually running an election campaign that never ends. In short, today we need to be a brand or business worth voting for. And that is where things go much deeper, since it then becomes grounded in values, beliefs, and behaviours over time.

There's a reason why Toyota was able to sustain their brand appeal despite accelerator issues and customer complaints. It's because they had years of positive equity in the bank. Likewise, regardless of any recent efforts by Air Canada to gain customer favour, they have years of poor customer services stories in their bank. Customer service in now inextricably linked to marketing. Marketing is now a listening job, not a telling job. And brands are simply narratives for your company's story as told by your customers.

How then will they tell your story? Will it be compelling and tied to your company values and the memorable behaviour of your employees? And more importantly, in the end, are you a brand worth voting for?

The Chemistry of Great Storytelling

. . .

While attending a recent parent-teacher interview, I drifted off momentarily while staring at the periodic table of elements on the wall. Perhaps still haunted by failed titration experiments, I reflected on how unnecessary it had all been in my current role as a marketing strategist. But then it hit me like only a thirty-year delayed learning outcome could. I realized in that moment that solids, liquids, and gases were great metaphors for traditional, social, and viral media campaigns. Stick with me here. I think I've found use for chemistry in marketing.

Perhaps on a subliminal level, I was reflecting on the BCAMA Vision Conference theme this year being 'liquid content', highlighting the concept of stories being told between web, mobile, TV, radio, print, outdoor, and more. Essentially winning campaigns now strive to use cross-platform storytelling rather than creating content for a particular medium.

Back to chemistry for a moment. We know solids are rigid, containing particles with little free space, which are locked in place. Solids are like traditional media. We can buy, measure, and control them, refining a combination of vehicles to target a defined segment of the market.

Liquids can move, containing particles that slide past one another, with little free space between them. They spread and assume the shape of the container they occupy. Liquids are that state of transition where campaign messages flow into storytelling across a variety of media, both traditional as well as electronic.

Gases contain particles that move and slide with lots of free space between them. They are compressible, but ultimately prefer to be free. Gases are that final stage of transition where having moved through solid and liquid phases, the airborne message has gone viral and moves about freely, uninhibited by word of mouth.

Perhaps this is why we can say that great campaigns start with good chemistry. They utilise the seamless transition between solid traditional, liquid electronic and social, and ultimately become gaseous word of mouth to effectively combine multiple media platforms into rich storytelling.

Okanagan Springs Brewery was a regional brand with a limited budget. They decided to sponsor small private events such as 'Jeff's weekend fishing trip' rather than large corporate events like most national beer brands. The campaign started with traditional newspaper and radio ads driving people to the sponsormespring.ca website where they could submit a video requesting sponsorship of their event. Visitors to the site were encouraged to vote for the events that they felt deserved sponsorship. Of course social media efforts by hopeful applicants further fuelled the word of mouth on the campaign. Sponsorships were handed out monthly to the events with the most votes and those deemed worthy of free beer and supplies. The events themselves then became the ad campaign with photos being used on billboards and print ads, and recorded audio became radio spots. While there was a fluid mixed use of traditional, electronic, and social media, arguably the unique storytelling element is what gave the campaign legs to achieve word-of-mouth viral success (http://creativity-online.com/work/okanagan-spring-brewery-sponsor-me-spring-case-study/17049).

Challenged with telling people about the upcoming 'Treasures Exhibit', **Science World** affixed two ounces of real 22-carat gold on the surface of a single billboard in downtown Vancouver and stamped it with a message about the show. While the value of the gold hammered micro thin was estimated at $11,000—and the price of media placement for four weeks added significantly to that, as well as the work involved to actually create the billboard—the value it achieved in traditional newspaper, TV, and radio publicity coverage as well as social media and viral storytelling was priceless. One simple idea combined with one traditional media billboard spawned an irresistible story that was shared across multiple fluid platforms and ultimately went viral (http://www.youtube.com/watch?v=NKhf-tH6PdI).

On some level, all companies are telling a story. Consumers live and move seamlessly through different media environments in their day-to-day lives. Having your story follow and interact in different modes along the way makes it more compelling and a natural fit in their lives. And ultimately, when you do that, it becomes more shareable. In the end, it really is all about the 'chemistry of good storytelling'.

2012 Social Media Marketing Industry Report

Recently 3,800 marketers targeting both B2B and B2C segments were surveyed for the 2012 Social Media Marketing Industry report. Among the insights?

1. The top question marketers still want answered: *How do I measure the effect of social media on my business?*
2. The top benefits of using social media: *85% use it to increase exposure (the no. 1 benefit), 69% said it increased traffic, 65% use it to provide marketplace insights.*
3. The top 5 social media tools being used: *Facebook, Twitter, LindedIn, blogs, YouTube (in that order).*
4. The amount of time being spent on social media: *59% said they use social media 6 or more hours per week. 33% said they invest 11 or more hours per week.*
5. The social media tool marketers want to learn more about: *Google+, introduced in late 2011 and currently used by 40% of marketers, was a significant insight here with 70% saying they want to learn more about how to use Google+ in their marketing efforts.*

There are tons more insights, including correlations of time spent and benefits realized, as well as drill-down information for businesses using social media specifically in a B2B or B2C application. Download the entire report for yourself here: http://www.socialmediaexaminer.com/social-media-marketing-industry-report-2012/.

Post, Pin, and Promote; Public versus Private Posts: Taking Advantage of Facebook Timeline Changes

. . .

This original article appeared one year ago. I have left it in its entirety, and then reflect at the end on changes that have happened since then.

April 4, 2012, marks the date when Facebook's Timeline features will kick in for those who have not voluntarily made the change. While this date may pass by unceremoniously for some, it will mark a dramatic change in how to best use Facebook for marketing efforts. Here are four changes you should take note of:

1. Pinning your posts

How it works: Pinned posts are page posts that you have chosen to display prominently at the top of your page. Pinned posts will remain there for 7 days, and after that they will return to the date they were posted in your timeline. Here's a quick video on how to pin a post: http://socialmediatravelers.com/how-to-pin-a-post-to-the-top-of-your-facebook-page

Why you should care: Now you can ensure content that positions you or your business is always what a visitor will see first. Although you might see all your posts as invaluable, you can now ensure the more trivial will not burry your gems.

2. Public post capability

How it works: Previously all Facebook posts were made to your 'friends'. Now you have the option of posting to different groups such as friends, close friends, other groups you may create, or to the public. When you post to the public, your content becomes viewable to anyone on the Internet and it is searchable. Managed well, this represents an opportunity for some. Here's a video on how to change who views your posts: http://www.youtube.com/watch?v=oDyVCGC_vvk.

Why you should care: Posting publicly presents an opportunity to position yourself as an expert or authority. Public posts become content that Google and other search engines catalogue and rank. This is an invaluable tool for branding and increasing awareness.

3. Timeline

How it works: All posts from the past and going forward will now be indexed by year and month. Timeline also allows you to go back to old posts and highlight or hide them.

Why you should care: Timeline presents a marketing opportunity for you or your brand to tell your story. You can 'go back in time' and post milestones that help give your brand a distinct identity.

4. Customized profile and cover banner photo

How it works: Previously Facebook users had a single profile photo. Now you will have both a profile photo and a cover banner photo that spans the entire top visual space of the page just like a website.

Why you should care: The cover banner image presents a branding and positioning opportunity. It can demonstrate your area of expertise, highlight what you care about, and in general, create a more personal connection.

You should also note the changes to your privacy settings after the April 4 update. By default, your past posts will have gone to timeline and they will be public, unless you change the settings. The good news is you can do a blanket change to make them all viewable to only friends again if you wish, make that your default going forward, or you can selectively decide which ones to delete or keep private. You can also preview what information is public versus viewable by friends. Here is a good video link to show you how to do all that: http://ansonalex.com/tutorials/how-to-prepare-your-facebook-profile-for-the-timeline-update/.

Bottom line? The changes that Facebook has made are significant. Managed well, they represent a significant opportunity.

An update for readers: The ability to post publicly has significantly helped boost search results, thus rendering the feature quite useful for businesses looking to create a digital footprint online. The Timeline feature also appears to be a useful tool to tell a business story over time—an essential feature of creating word of mouth, mouse, and mobile!

Big, Battered, Bruised, and Back for More: Learning from Social Media Mistakes of Big Global Brands

. . .

What can we learn from the social media screw-ups of the biggest global brands? Lots. Their mistakes can teach the rest of us some valuable lessons. Facebook, Twitter, and YouTube have 1.2 billion combined users. That's a lot of influence for media vehicles that didn't exist prior to 2005. And that doesn't even include the countless blogs and other social media tools and apps out there. Simply put, the marketplace has the ability to correct wrongs now like no other time in history. Three areas stand out as themes for summarizing these stumbles:

Photo: Mary Charleson

1. **Connect and amplify:** Social media gives customers the ability to connect with others who are sharing similar problems and to then amplify their concerns online. It would seem that airlines have fallen from grace repeatedly here, but any company in the business of providing service to large numbers of customers should be wary. **JetBlue Airlines** created their own hostage crisis (never a good word in the airline industry) on February 14, 2007 (Valentine's Day, not a good day to say, 'We don't love you') when passengers were stranded for eleven hours in a plane on the tarmac. Several filmed their experience. One started a blog. It went viral (http://www.nytimes.com/2007/02/17/business/17air.html). What ensued were groups of passengers who started sharing their experiences with delays and poor treatment. In the end, JetBlue issued a public apology via social media.

   In February 2010, **Southwest Airlines** removed a customer from a flight because he was taking up more space than the one seat he had paid for. Admittedly large, Kevin Smith, the offender, was outraged. He took to blogging and tweeting his experience. Perhaps Southwest should have checked his 'online influence' before hastily removing him, since Kevin was a US filmmaker with considerable followers and media ties. Couple that with an empathetic US population where many are overweight, and the potential to connect and amplify was immense—to pardon the pun (http://www.guardian.co.uk/film/2010/feb/15/overweight-filmmaker-banned-southwest-airlines).

   When **United Airlines** trashed Dave Carroll's guitar through mishandling it, he tried for close to a year to get compensated and finally turned his frustration into a song and video that became a YouTube sensation (http://www.youtube.com/watch?v=5YGc4zOqozo). His experience united numerous others who chimed in with similar stories of mishandled and damaged luggage.

2. **Highlight hidden problems:** Beware the security camera. Especially when they are in the hands of every single one of your customers poised to instantly share your company indiscretions online with millions. That's the lesson learned by **FedEx** when a video of an employee tossing a package over a fence rather than delivering it to the door went viral on YouTube. Can we assume the employee couldn't read that the package was a computer monitor? Both the video and the customer's plight of having the damaged product replaced haunted FedX online for months afterwards (http://www.youtube.com/watch?v=PKUDTPbDhnA). Not to be left in the delivery dust, **UPS** was also captured handling parcels less than delicately (http://www.youtube.com/watch?v=qGCdOmykOOg&feature=player_embedded). These viral hits have spawned a plethora of 'me too' videos with countless customers sharing similar experiences.

3. **Creative misfires:** Sometimes social media can be a big think tank to correct ill thought out creative platforms. Consider these attempts to offend moms and dads in two different efforts. When **Motrin** launched their commercial for pain relief, targeted at new moms during national baby-carrying week, they didn't anticipate a backlash against the creative theme that poked fun at them feeling 'tired and crazy'. But offend it did. Boycotts were arranged and ad parodies posted. It wasn't until the story of how **Johnson & Johnson** had missed the mark, and apparently were not monitoring the social media comments, hit mainstream media that the ad was pulled. Recently, **Kimberly-Clark**, the makers of **Huggies Diapers**, met the wrath of dads, tired of being portrayed as incompetent dumb fathers, with a commercial to show a diaper meant to rise to the ultimate challenge of not being changed for hours in the 'Huggies Dad test'. While women may well find the commercial funny, arguably the growing number of dads engaged in parenting should have led the company to consider the

shifts that have taken place in their target market and to consider the creative accordingly.

There are really three lessons to be learned here:

1. If you fail to understand your target market, social media will let you know. Do your research.
2. If you have core business service problems, they need to be solved. If you don't, they will blow up online.
3. Don't play in social media unless you are going to monitor and manage feedback. Dedicate resources and do it well.

How Will Facebook's New Timeline Tell Your Story?

■ ■ ■

While I have obviously since migrated to Timeline, I have presented this article as it first appeared to reflect on what the changes meant at the time and how best to utilise them to your advantage now.

Like many of you, I have been receiving banner alerts when logging into **Facebook**, prompting me to migrate to the new Timeline and banner design. I've noted numerous colleagues who have made the switch, and I've also been touring pages looking for creative approaches. I've yet to make the change since I am currently analyzing what is driving it and how to best use the new platform look to position not only my business page, but also my own personal brand. I do think it demands some pre-thought, since the page will now look much more like a 'personal or brand website' with the banner on the top, and most importantly, the timeline feature presenting the opportunity to 'tell your story' for brands and individuals.

Since 'resistance is futile' (for you Trek fans), with a default migration date of March 30 for all accounts, I think it's prudent to consider the opportunities that the new design presents, rather than just allowing a blanket switch to be tripped on your behalf.

The first obvious change is the opportunity to tell your story chronologically with an emphasis on visuals. Storytelling is powerful. Attention needs to be paid to structure, highlights, headlines, and images. Done well, Timeline could present a powerful social narrative that creates an emotional connection for brands or individuals. You can now **create milestones** to emphasize important events or hide old content to control how it appears. You can also go back and insert content and change your history (if that feels like a time warp, it is!) But again, if you are narrating the evolution of a brand or showing an illustrious history, this is powerful stuff. This is not something to leave to a default migrating tool to select highlights for your story.

Pinned posts are another opportunity. You can now 'pin a post' and place it at the top of your feed for a week as a highlight to your followers. This presents an incredible opportunity for businesses that feed their multimedia social media content such as videos and blog posts regularly via Facebook. This feature definitely favours those who publish content regularly. I suspect that is at the heart of this, since Facebook benefits by encouraging active use of the platform, and by default, they will further enrich their database on you as a user. That will translate to sellable user profiling for advertising.

The new **Reach Generator tool** is also at the heart of these changes and is closely tied to the pinned post concept. Businesses will be able to use it to help promote posts to existing fans via newsfeeds and the mobile web. Of course the monetization of this tool presents increased revenue for Facebook. Link here for more background on the Reach Generator tool: http://techcrunch. com/2012/03/04/facebook-marketing-conference/.

Starbucks has done a nice job migrating to the new look while utilizing the Timeline tool to feature company milestones and product launches since 1971. The retro look of old photos really adds to the style and presentation (https://www.facebook.com/ Starbucks?fref=ts). **The *New York Times*** has also created an interesting historical perspective on not only their company, but also on newsworthy historical events (http://www.facebook.com/ nytimes?ref=ts).

Sprott-Shaw College has also made the switch, although the content between 1903 and current day is sparse. Seems like a missed opportunity to position their private school brand uniquely amidst their competitors, since they actually have history that pre-dates UBC (https://www.facebook.com/sprottshaw?fref=ts). Those are a couple examples of what I found, but curiously, a lot of top brands haven't switched over. I will be monitoring them closely for creative approaches in the coming months.

As with good writing and storytelling, you need to consider your audience when addressing these changes. How will you 'frame' your story through photos, tags, and highlight milestones? This is where I am still perplexed as to how best to utilise Timeline. While Facebook has enabled easier 'groups' to share your posts with, they haven't considered this wrinkle when designing Timeline. The story I would choose to tell friends and family might be quite different than the one I would highlight to clients and business colleagues. This is where having a personal Facebook identity as well as a business page might finally make the most sense.

One last thought on all this. As a parent, I would encourage you to help your kids understand how Timeline is now part of their personal branding and identity. The implications are profound when you consider how colleges, universities, and future employers may use the tool to screen candidates. Most are writing for their current 'audience of buddies and friends', and the content they highlight on their Timeline may not serve them well in the future. By engaging Facebook, we now have no choice but to also play the personal branding game.

So take a tour and become familiar with the new tools. Then consider how best to utilise them to your advantage. Map out a plan for your business or personal brand, then log in and tell your story. And finally, consider how in the future you will use the new tools to position yourself favourably.

Should ROI Be the Only Measure of Social Media Success?

∎ ∎ ∎

Some have heralded 2012 as the year that social media will move from infatuation akin to dating in an early relationship and mature to something more of a permanent partnership, but one that is assessed objectively for attributes and value.

Along with that move to partnership, it is said, will come demands for ROI (return on investment) and, in particular, a more sophisticated approach to measuring engagement and ultimately sales conversion. Sounds like it's all about the money, honey. But should it be?

Is it really time to assess this partner only on the nuts and bolts results that it can deliver to the cash register? Sort of feels like assessing that prospective partner for their ability to be a stable provider only, rather than considering all other facets of the relationship. Surely in the era of engagement and consumer brand influence, there is more at stake. Building brand equity takes time. It can be hard to measure. It's kind of like trying to attach a value to a conversation. You can't do it. You can't buy a conversation, but you can surely provoke, engage, or respond to one online. Arguably that conversation over time adds value to your brand. But does it generate immediate sales? Not necessarily, and that's the point.

ROI and celebrating sales figures is an activity done quarterly and annually. Brand equity, share of mind, and share of heart are not so tidily and timely delivered. But where there is share of heart, share of pocketbook is bound to follow.

Only 17% of Businesses Contribute to and Monitor Social Media Regularly

■ ■ ■

According to a recent Leger Marketing survey, 17% of large and mid-sized companies consistently post on social media sites or monitor them. That means that, by default, 83% are not using or monitoring social media. That number should scare you, especially if your business falls into the latter group. Also consider that 51% of social media users post negative feedback.

What makes social media feedback so toxic to ignore is the fact that it sits in a public space for others to see, potentially spurring on additional negative feedback. The traditional complaint process saw the issue sit in a customer service representative's inbox or voicemail, where frankly it could be easily ignored, or at the very least, dealt with in a non-urgent manner. Today with the power of social media on their side, consumers are empowered to get timely attention and resolution. Companies are especially apt to respond quickly if that person has a significant digital footprint and influence on social media with lots of friends on Facebook or a significant Twitter following.

As an experiment, I decided to use socialmention.com, a free social media monitoring site to search comments being made about prominent companies. Knowing airlines are an easy target for service screw-ups, I started with Air Canada. Within minutes, I had found a fellow who had posted to his Facebook page less than kind words about his inability to get a drink while waiting in the Platinum lounge due to a delayed flight. A quick check revealed he had over 1,800 friends on Facebook whom he had shared his comment with. Within twenty minutes of the comment being made, he had over twelve responses, all supporting his negative views. Another quick check revealed this fellow had an even more significant following on Twitter. In the end, I suspect he went thirsty in the lounge of social media monitoring, since his occupation was listed as tattoo artist from California. But what if he had been a Fortune 500 CEO or major business user? Frankly, tattoo artist or not, the fact that he was entitled to the Platinum lounge and he had a significant following should have meant someone tagged the comment and followed up with him.

However, we do know that major companies such as Air Canada are now employing social media representatives, and they do follow and deal with online comments. Just ask Virginia Sokoloff, a disgruntled customer who had her flight accidentally cancelled by an Air Canada rep and had to actually buy a new ticket for over $700 to get home. Her complaints at the service counter went unresolved, as did her phone calls several days later. But her Facebook wall posting received an immediate response and she was offered a refund and discount on future flights. The fact she had a significant following on Facebook likely played in that decision.

Although it's easy to take the nick out of airlines, all businesses that serve customers should be aware of the potential damage to their brand that can result from a social media conversation to which they are not privy or choose to not participate.

Curious about how you business might stack up? Wonder about your competitors? Visit www.socialmention.com and plug in a few key words. It will search the universe of social media and deliver you links to comments, as well as give you a measure of whether those comments are positive, negative, or neutral. And it's absolutely free!

P2P (People to People) Strategy Important in Age of Social Media

■ ■ ■

I teach undergraduate and graduate level university marketing courses. Current textbooks are filled with strategies for B2B (business to business) and B2C (business to consumer) applications. But I really think with the evolution of social media and its impact on business, both of these areas have evolved into a P2P (people to people) model.

Why P2P?

People do business with people. They become friends with people. They form an emotional connection with people. Few businesses exist without some personal contact. In the new world of social media, the people who work for you and the people who have bought from you have a voice.

Yet many businesses are uncertain how to best use social media. They fear exposure. They don't know how to hand negative comments. They fret about the time spent to manage social media. Their fear is based largely on losing control.

Let's take a look at a good and bad example P2P marketing in action in the age of social media.

Dave Carroll is a Canadian musician who had his Taylor guitar damaged beyond repair due to extreme negligence while flying United Airlines. After being given the runaround for close to a year, trying to make a claim for replacement against the airline, he took to YouTube. He recorded an entertaining video and catchy tune that told the tale of mistreatment by the airline. It became a viral hit, currently with 11.5 million views worldwide. Watch it here: http://www.youtube.com/watch?v=5YGc4zOqozo.

Within two days of the video hitting the airwaves, United offered him compensation. But Dave wasn't finished. He went on to produce a total of three videos about how the company handled the exchange. He now makes a living as a musician and speaker advocating for good customer service and educating companies about how to handle social media complaints.

Virginia Sokolloff, of Montreal, felt she was mistreated by Air Canada when her outbound flight was first cancelled, then had her return ticket voided while being issued a new flight. She was forced to buy a new ticket for over $700. The additional $25 baggage charge was the final straw. But instead of taking to the phone, Ms Sokoloff took to Facebook, posting her story not only on her own personal page, but also on Air Canada's Facebook page. Within minutes of posting on the airline's wall, a social media representative from the airline contacted her. She was offered a refund for her ticket and a discount on a future booking.

Two airlines and two different outcomes. Company bureaucracy guided one. The other allowed a person-to-person exchange and employee empowerment to make a wrong a right. Arguably that should have been done at the ticket counter without having to resort to social media, but at least they got it half right.

Many businesses are still learning about monitoring social media. The leaders will be the ones who empower their employees to make decisions on the spot and treat customers with respect, just like a friend would.

Good relationships are transparent. There is little to hide, and each partner responds to the other in a timely manner with attention and respect. And they each realize that all humans have some flaws. It's what makes them personable.

P2P (people to people) strategy is the new world order. I invite you to pause for a moment and consider the implications for your business. Perhaps you have a story of how social media played a role dealing with a complaint?

The New Loyalty Loop Marketing Model

■ ■ ■

What possible commonality could a previously unpublished writer now making over $200,000/month selling e-books on Amazon share with the makers of a head-shaving helmet and an expensive Super Bowl ad spoof for Groupon? Admittedly a motley crew to lump together, they all have benefited or suffered under economics of the new *loyalty loop* that the Internet has brought to marketing.

In December 2010, **Harvard Business Review** published an article called 'Branding in the Digital Age: You're Spending Your Money in All the Wrong Places'. Since reading the article, I've found myself constantly re-evaluating how consumer decisions are influenced. We have moved from the traditional funnel of consistently narrowing our choices from many to fewer and finally a purchase, and are now moving towards the loyalty loop where choices are added and subtracted during an extended consideration and evaluation phase, then once a purchase is made, we openly share, exchange, and advocate while fuelling the influence of others online.

Allow me to elaborate with my three unusual examples to illustrate the power of the loyalty loop.

1. **The long tail economics of successful indie writers selling e-books online.** Twenty-six-year-old Amada Hocking (http://amandahocking.blogspot.com/) has self-published eight novels online since April 2010 and currently averages sales of 100,000 e-books/month through Amazon. Top Kindle indie authors typically sell 2,500-

100,000 books/month, with many in the 10,000 range. At an average of $3/book, and Amazon taking 30%, the remaining profit looks pretty sweet. Sell books at a low-risk, low-price point to lots of people. This model is only possible with the *loyalty loop marketing model*. It's one thing to write and publish an e-book. It's quite another to actually cultivate a following online to generate those kind of sale numbers. Amanda tweets and is well connected in the blogging community where she sends advanced reading copies to influential book bloggers. Her urban fantasy and romance appeals to youth. Readers and the connected blog community advocate and feed the loyalty loop, which in turn influences more buyers online. Recently her success has garnered TV and magazine stories (http://www.youtube.com/watch?v=1qWOy4p4MvM). She doesn't pay a cent for marketing.

2. **Groupon's Super Bowl Tibet ad blunder.** Of course the loyalty loop can work in reverse. Advocacy can turn negative, as it did following Groupon's attempt at self-inflicted humour. In case you missed it, Groupon paid over $1 million for a thirty-second spot during the Super Bowl. In it, actor Timothy Hutton appears to make light of the political struggle in Tibet in the name of a great Groupon deal at a Tibetan restaurant. Supposedly they were making fun of themselves talking about discounts as a noble cause, and viewers having seen humour in the parody would appreciate the philanthropic donation that Groupon had set up for Tibet. Too bad the connecting website never appeared in the ad. And too bad the great unwashed tuned into Super Bowl were largely more receptive to crass objectification of women in their advertising than obtuse connections. So how did the new *loyalty loop marketing model* fail them? Arguably much of the value of purchasing a Super Bowl ad goes beyond the high reach of the TV audience. Chatter before, during, and after the event online is where the real value is. In Groupon's

case, they didn't frame the spot before to build anticipation and understanding, and then they failed to respond quickly afterwards. They dropped the ball where the loyalty loop mattered most—online. Talk turned negative and they never really recovered.

3. **Headblade's crazy shaving helmet video.** So you're a small company that designs and sells razors to a highly targeted segment—people who shave their heads. How do you let the world know your razor is the best? You create a hokey-looking home-made video demonstrating a helmet that when worn will lather and shave your head with motorized razors in about thirty seconds. Sound scary? Sound unbelievable? This YouTube viral video marketing campaign was fresh, edgy, and most importantly, sparked conversations about head shaving (http://www.youtube.com/watch?v=5bgRszdUdhQ). It featured one of their razors in the helmet and demonstrated how it works. The helmet, later revealed as a hoax, actually generated countless purchase enquiries for the company. The online chatter grew exponentially and flooded over to mainstream media. The company experienced record hits to their website where they featured the real products they sell (http://www.headblade.com/). In the *loyalty loop marketing model*, they gained incredibly positive traction in a rather obscure category.

So the big question to ask is this: is your marketing feeding the marketing funnel or the loyalty loop?

Sages on Stage
with Predictions for 2011

■ ■ ■

Recently I attended a **BC Chapter of the American Marketing Association** breakfast meeting to hear what an advertising agency panel had to say about strategies for 2011. Judging by the three-hundred-plus people in the room at an early hour, the promise of a sage on the stage to enlighten was attractive. It could also be that many are both anxious and excited about the changes unfolding. Predictably social media dominated the conversation, but a few themes emerged:

1. **The traditional model of unearthing the 'big idea', then using push media and repetition to gain recognition is over.** Launch and leave is simply not as effective in an age of social media. Agencies now need to monitor and manage a brand. Call it nurturing the garden, not just planting the seeds. This is challenging both the way ideas are approached and executed as well as how agencies get compensated.

2. **Social media needs something to talk about, which makes storytelling even more relevant.** Start your story in one media and then extend it to another. Stephan Hawes, managing director, TBWA Vancouver, coined the term 'transmedia' as a new approach to integrating communications, where each media gets a piece of the message and consumers are allowed to put it together by engaging and exchanging. Lance Saunders, executive vice

president, managing director, DDB, suggests, 'We need to create a story where people can insert themselves.'

3. **Accept that you may no longer be in control.** New social media tools, in the hands of consumers, have changed the power relationship. However, a powerful insight emerges: people trust people. The less control you have over your marketing, the more credibility you will have. Saunders suggests, 'Stop, listen, and lasso the conversations that matter to your target and engage them.'

4. **Mobile is very important for some markets.** Although penetration of smartphones is still small overall, it is significant for some audiences, such as small business and millennials. Neilson Online reports 5 million Canadians using mobile devices to access the internet in 2010. By 2014, half of Internet impressions are expected to be off mobile devices. That may change the content, context, and interactivity considerations for your website.

5. **Traditional media is not dead.** Media such as print and TV are still big and relevant; however, there is no doubting that PVRs pose a threat to commercial viewing, and tablets like the iPad threaten how print content is delivered and paid for. But consider the success of the Old Spice commercials and subsequent engagement online through Facebook and Twitter with custom video responses to an online audience. They spend handsomely on a TV campaign initially to reach a mass audience. Then the online component kicked in. They gave people something to talk about and then selectively engaged certain conversations. Flash back to points 2 and 3.

6. **If the idea is king, data is queen.** I have to give credit for that line to Tom Shepansky, founding partner, Rethink. ROI is driving decisions, and the increased influence of digital and social media means that IT is at the creative table. He suggests hiring 'digital citizens' (those under 30 who have grown up immersed in this stuff) to train the 'digital immigrants' (those over 40 who think they're

knowledgeable, but secretly go to bed every night afraid of what they *don't* know).

The **Harvard Business Review** published an article in December 2010 called 'Branding in the Digital Age: You're Spending Your Money in All the Wrong Places'. Do yourself a favour and read it. Research based, this article challenges the traditional funnel of consumer decision-making process. It reveals how we have moved to a loyalty loop, which profoundly changes where advertising messaging should be placed. Marketing textbooks will be re-written. I made it mandatory reading for my students.

Of course with any good forecast session, the usual caveats prevailed. Noted Saunders at the end of his presentation, 'On the other hand, I could be totally off.' Indeed, but not far off.

Are You Unsocial by Being so Social?

∎ ∎ ∎

The new shiny toy gets all the hype. It's the one that gets talked about, wished for, and idolized. It promises to be better, stronger, and faster. It replaces those before it in the glance that it takes to rip the paper from its cover. Many shiny toys of Christmas past are still with us. Some with fifty-year staying power like Barbie, never really having fallen far from favour. Others were a simple flash-in-the-pan fad, befallen and buried with pet rocks and mood rings.

Social media is our new shiny toy. But far from a fad, it represents a fundamental shift in the way consumers communicate. At the root of social media are online creating, sharing, and connecting. It's like one big cocktail party where other people get to talk about you. The key of course is that although you may provoke a conversation, you cannot control it. It is a conversation that everyone at the party believes holds more truth than what you would say yourself or pay to be able to tell others. That is the fundamental difference, and ultimately the power that it holds.

Let's consider some facts:

- 34% of bloggers post opinions about products and brands.
- 20% of tweets contain a reference to a product or brand.
- 78% of consumers trust pier recommendations. Only 14% trust advertising.
- 56% of journalists said social media was important when reporting stories. 89% use blogs when conducting online research.

- 45%% of mobile handsets are smartphones, further enabling all of these activities in real time and location based. That is up from 31% just one year prior.

Clearly, social media and mobile platforms is where the future of media and advertising is headed.

Or is it? With so much emphasis on social media—utilizing Twitter, Facebook, YouTube, Foursquare, and blogs, and monitoring or updating all this activity with tools like Nutshell, Hootsuite, or Tweetdeck, I fear we may risk becoming 'unsocial by being so social'. I sense an infatuation with the new shiny toy right now that I suspect will settle as we figure out what tool to use when and for what audience.

Consider a campaign running right now for Shaw home phone. It cuts through the clutter by suggesting we use a phone to talk. This simple creative insight shows how far we have migrated. The inference is that rather than announce a new job or grandchild on Facebook or Twitter, that hearing the refreshing ring of a voice call on a phone and the suggestion that 'what they really want is to hear the sound of your voice' is powerful. BBDO is the agency responsible for the creative. This campaign is running on radio and TV right now. It uses traditional media, with a creative insight that connects with the target customer. And there's not an ounce of social in sight. Brilliant.

I conducted an experiment at a convention I recently spoke at. I was talking about marketing with an emphasis on new media. Attendees would naturally expect e-mails, newsletters, hashtags on Twitter and the like as my promotional tools of choice. So when I sent them a Vancouver postcard in advance, by mail, hand-addressed with a personal note inviting them to the breakout session, they were understandably intrigued. Most arrived with the card in hand, and the session was packed. I had to do some negotiation with the convention organizers to have them mail the card on my behalf for privacy reasons. The gesture was unexpected, got attention, and cut through the clutter. I was quickly able to dispel any notions of being a dinosaur with my traditional approach. Most appreciated it for what it was, a clever plot to have them attend. Who wouldn't read a personally addressed, handwritten postcard from the most beautiful place on earth?

Now I'm hardly suggesting that you walk away from social media. Far from it. I am however suggesting that you look critically at your objective and your target audience. In our rush to be social with social media, we risk becoming unsocial for some projects and targets. You want to achieve a connection with your customer. Choose your tool wisely—new and shiny, or not.

Going Viral

▪ ▪ ▪

Do you know who was born on May 14, 2005? While they are now just eight years old, they have in a short time changed the way we communicate and share information as global citizens. If you guessed **YouTube**, you are correct. Acquired by **Google** in 2006, YouTube quickly has become *the* vehicle for sharing online video with mass audiences. It has also quickly become a major tool for viral advertising messages, essentially content created with the intent that consumers will share it with others and help spread the message. This 'consumer to consumer' model rather than 'business to consumer' is a key to the success of social media.

You're likely familiar with some of the most widely viewed shared viral spots: **Dove's 'Evolution'** (http://www.youtube.com/watch?v=iYhCn0jf46U), one of the first truly viral campaigns featuring the girl next door turning into a fashion beauty through makeup and photo retouching. Launched in 2006, it has garnered over 11 million views. You may have been one of the 25 million who viewed the **Evian 'Roller Babies'** (http://www.youtube.com/watch?v=XQcVllWpwGs) featuring digitally manipulated roller-skating infants. While most online commercials were created for TV and then garnered a second life online, the Evian spot was created exclusively for online sharing. Make no mistake, the costs they saved in a TV media buy were easily exceeded in the production of the spot, but it is one of the first commercials created for online that, due to its success, is now being aired on TV. We could go on: **'Charlie bit my finger'** is a piece of home movie featuring two British toddlers, now at 299 million views; **Susan Boyle**, the frumpy singing sensation on *Britain's Got*

Talent, now at 95 million views. It becomes quickly evident that pieces that are shared by e-mail, **Twitter, Facebook**, or linked to and blogged about have a number of things in common. For those who would like to use social media, and **YouTube** in particular, as a marketing driver, here is a list of five things you should consider to increase the likelihood of your video going viral.

1. **Humour works.** Let's face it, there's enough disaster and drama in the world. If we can view something that brightens our day, and better yet, share it with others, the chances are good that we will.
2. **Stir emotions.** If you can't make them laugh, then make them cry. Or at least tear up long enough to feel compelled to share it with others who need a good emotional outburst. Women love to share online content with other women. Emotional content can be a major touchpoint.
3. **Keep it short.** Although your online video needn't be limited to the traditional thirty-second or one-minute commercial length, many successful videos are, simply because that is the medium they were originally created for. This has programmed us as to what we will sit through before seeking the next bit of entertainment. Call it the plague of a severely attention deficit disordered generation.
4. **Headlines matter. Make your title catchy.** The sound bite generation wants entertainment to grab their attention. A play on words, a sensationalized promise, or anything that begs 'I have to see this' response is what you're after.
5. **Keep it simple.** One single and simple message will create maximum impact.

Finally, understand that parodies can be both good and bad. If you can create your own parody of a well-known spot to somehow profile your own brand, you can springboard off the popularity of the original. **Specsavers** in the UK did a very successful parody of an **Axe** ad for men's deodorant featuring bikini-clad women flocking to a guy spraying himself with Axe on the beach. Only when he dons some cheesy glasses and sees the ultimate male fantasy unfolding before him is he revealed as the geek who should have visited Specsavers. Watch the original here: http://www.youtube.com/watch?v=I9tWZB7OUSU. View the parody here: http://www.youtube.com/watch?v=VvpO4Ll-rXg.

If you somehow become the object of a parody, make sure you have people monitoring the online world and respond selectively if at all. The way you handle this public relations challenge will be critical. **Motrin** learned this the hard way with their ad aimed at moms with backaches that carry their children in baby slings. Here's the ad: http://www.youtube.com/watch?v=BmykFKjNpdY. Link to some of the controversy here:http://parenting.blogs.nytimes.com/2008/11/17/moms-and-motrin/?_r=1.

Word of Mouth, Mouse, and Mobile

• • •

I teach a media course at one of our local universities. Recently I brought some newspapers in to my class for the students to look at. My father was a 'newspaper historian' and had saved papers from noteworthy events over time such as the *Halifax Chronicle* the day WW11 ended, and the *Toronto Star* marking man's first walk on the moon and Paul Henderson's goal.

I watched with fascination as these twenty-somethings approached the papers like historical artifacts. There was confusion over the Radio Shack 8-track player ad and disbelief at the Vancity ad for 15.5% interest rates in the '80s.

Why the fascination? Papers of this size and editorial detail were a foreign experience for them. They were a generation that gets their information primarily from digital means.

This story is relevant for marketers today for a number of reasons. There's a fundamental shift taking place. Marketing is a 'lagging' indicator. It follows the places people spend their time— and they are increasingly spending more time with digital.

Forrester Research recorded some interesting comparisons in a September 2009 poll. The amount of time we are spending with digital media is increasing, but the per cent of marketing budgets being spent on it has not kept up. Thirty-four per cent of our time is spent on the Internet, yet only 12% of advertising spending is allocated there. In contrast, TV viewing was 35% and commanded 31% of marketing budgets.

There are three stages consumers go through when purchasing: brand awareness, brand consideration, and brand purchase. Digital has been good at facilitating the first and last steps. Search ads, blogs, and e-mails are used to create awareness just like ads. E-commerce has made purchases quick, easy, and available to worldwide markets. But the real opportunity, and where we're seeing a fundamental shift, is in the middle—the consideration and preference stage. This is where people seek out information and reasons to buy. This is the stage where word of mouth, mouse, and mobile are very important.

Word of mouth is human nature. People love to share stories. Word of mouse is a logical progression in a world with readily available wireless and 24/7 computer access. We pass a lot of information on to others via our computers. But it's the word of mobile that is about to explode. Soon smartphones like the iPhone and Blackberry will be the only phone style available. Once that happens, everyone will have the Internet on their hip or in their pierce all the time. And that is going to change how we approach marketing.

Let's take a look at an example to illustrate.

Who knew our prime minister could play the piano? Few. But that all changed after an October performance at the National Arts Centre Gala. He practiced for a week and didn't tell anyone. His handlers only found out about it two days before and actually tried to stop it—fearing a Stockwell Day wetsuit fiasco. The video was shot on an iPhone by an audience member and posted to YouTube. Another audience member with 612 followers scanned YouTube and then tweeted about it during the concert. It then spread virally online via texts, e-mail, tweets, social networking sites. Mainstream media picked it up. Within three days, it was the third highest viewed video on YouTube worldwide with over 500,000 views. View it here: http://www.youtube.com/watch?v=JOt2Qp0H9G8.

Why did it work? **It was unexpected.** Few knew he could play and sing. Few thought he'd make himself vulnerable. **It was emotional.** He showed his human side. 'Getting By with a Little Help from My Friends' was in contrast to his distant, aloof façade. **It was authentic.** Although the event was planned, the way it spread was not. It was not spun. It just as easily could have bombed.

These three attributes—unexpected, emotional, and authentic—are key to having others spread your message for you. And that's the power of digital for marketers. These attributes are the basis of a good story and, come to think of it, what reporters have always looked for in traditional media. Maybe there's nothing new happening here at all, just a change of vehicle.

As my class of students, almost all with their smartphones, reminded me the digital world is our new reality. Welcome to the world of mouth, mouse, and mobile.

Tracking Social Media

. . .

This fall, Internet ad spending in the UK outpaced TV ad spending for the first time ever in history. TV ad spending commanded 22% and the Internet took up 24% of advertising expenditures. While some were quick to write the obituary for traditional media, the UK market is a bit of an anomaly with its restricted advertising on the BBC and an abundance of broadband penetration. However, it does signal a significant shift. Let's call it a disruption.

The number of Chinese Internet users now exceeds that of the US. That's 338 million Chinese web users to 308 million Americans. User penetration in the US is 70%. In China, it's 25% and increasing. Let's call that growth.

Advertising Age recently reported a 400% surge in mobile video uploads to YouTube largely attributable to new iPhones and the Blackberry. It is now clear that there is an inseparable link between social media and mobile devices. Let's call that opportunity.

So where does disruption, growth, and opportunity leave us? The Internet is big, but mobile media is bigger. Online advertising is important, but social media is critical. Both mobile and social media are good at reaching niche audiences and getting them actively engaged on a personal level. And that's the new part of the selling process that marketers are coming to grip with. In social media, it's about offering something of value, engaging passionate fans, and giving them the tools to influence others. It's not about pushing out a message or the number of exposures.

Interestingly, a whole new measurement mechanism is emerging to quantify social media. Infegy, a US-based firm, tracks 20 million web pages, including the leading social media sites such as Twitter, Facebook, Myspace, YouTube, and reports the per cent of positive mentions against overall brand mentions within social media in their monthly Social Radar Sentiment Index. They analyze online buzz by the sentence, rather than just counting the number of positive words in an effort to get an accurate read of whether mentions are positive or negative. The index focuses heavily on mega brands, but it offers a clear insight about what leading companies are doing.

Here's a few highlights from a recent report:

Apple beat Microsoft largely on the basis of its overwhelming conversation volume, generating more than 900,000 mentions in a month. However Microsoft still had the second highest volume of mentions. Despite much negative media coverage in the bailout-plagued auto industry, Ford had an 87.6% positive mention rate and General Motors had a 71.4% positive rating. And Dove generated more than 141,000 comments, 81.6% positive, still appearing to benefit from the 'Campaign for Real Beauty' and viral 'Evolution' video three years after it first appeared.

Leading brands are using social media to allow their customers to become their best advocates. Positive mentions are of course contingent on meeting and exceeding customer expectations and connecting with them on an emotional level. Perhaps this is where advertising dollars are best spent these days. Get good, facilitate talk, and then listen.

Social media aided by the growth of mobile devices is undoubtedly a disruption. But disruptions have happened before. The printing press disrupted oral communications. Radio and film disrupted newspapers and live theatre. TV in the 1950s disrupted radio. Cable TV and specialty channels in the '60s/'70s disrupted network TV. What is common with all these is this: The disruption fragmented the audience and caused new patterns of media consumption. However, the other thing that is common is that none of the previous communication vehicles went away. They simply took on a different role with a refined focus and purpose. That is a pattern worth noting.

Guerrilla Marketing Campaigns and Creating Public Relations Buzz

■ ■ ■

Traditional advertising such as print, broadcast, outdoor, and direct mail has taken a hit of late. It's a blow suffered at the hands of the new kid on the block, social media, and other online applications. There's infatuation with social media. Like a new romance, it is mysterious, intriguing, and hot. The difference however is, unlike a flaming summer romance, this new partnership is going to last. The reason? This new social media partner is thoughtful and likes to listen and share. They are not boastful and showy. And most of all, they are personal—forever at your side courtesy of the increasing proliferation of iPhones, Blackberrys, and other data devices. Traditional media are unlikely to go anywhere soon since they hold a tremendous amount of power and clout for getting a message out to the masses. But the secret will be to utilise the strengths of both traditional and new media in unison.

One interesting area in transition is the publicity stunt. Long a bastion of businesses in search of publicity and media coverage, what has changed is the effort to engage online chatter via social networks and blogs along with traditional TV, radio, and print media in the antics. Let's look at a couple of recent examples.

Think you've seen it all when it comes to clever delivery of advertising messages? Think again. Enter to latest human ad platform: *backvertising*. Take one very hairy man, carve out your message on his follicle-enhanced slate, and send him strolling down Kits Beach handing out Parissa Wax Strip samples. It was sure to be a head turner, and generate talk both on the beach and online, amongst the primary target market: beach-going men and women in search of a smooth body. The publicity stunt was the brainchild of Vancouver advertising agency Rethink for North Vancouver-based Parissa, a supplier of hair removal products throughout North America. Marketing and media types were given a heads-up to the exercise the day before through a teaser release and seeded mentions in various blogs and on Twitter. Here's a link to how this stunt generated online and offline interest: https://www.youtube.com/watch?v=MIxDPwyxsBc.

If you've been in a bar in Vancouver recently, you've likely seen a poster or drink coaster promoting the cell phone Breathalyzer. The service, available by calling 1-877-EZ-ALCO-TEST, instructs callers to blow into the cell phone microphone for a continuous five seconds. With the endless parade of gadgets and capabilities on cell phones these days, it's easy to see how, with a few drinks, this technology might seem plausible. Think again. Duped callers, following their breath test attempt, are met with the response, 'If you actually believe this works, you're probably drunk out of your mind and may require a designated driver; please call Keys Please at 1-866-586-5397. They'll dispatch a driver to get you home safely.' Calgar—based Keys Please operates in BC, Alberta, and Manitoba. Arguably better than any poster or ad campaign since it strikes at a moment of truth keeping drunks off the road, the surprising humour created a lot of buzz around Vancouver clubs via talk, text, and online groups. The non-traditional campaign won a gold at Canadian advertising industry Marketing Awards in June 2009. Rethink strikes again.

Aside from flat-out creativity and the ability to touch the target market in a meaningful and memorable way, these two campaigns achieved a coveted accomplishment: word of mouth and word of mouse. Third-party endorsement, from a trusted source, can be one of the most powerful advertising vehicles out there. Smart businesses will continue to strive for this in clever ways while utilizing social networks and online tools that give the message buzz. Social media as an engaged partner are here to stay. Expect to be seated with this summer romance at the Thanksgiving table for some time to come.

word of

M UTH
M USE &
M BILE

CHAPTER 2

Tracking Trends

. . .

Tracking trends is a significant element of an effective marketing strategy. Research can help you measure what's going on and, even more importantly, gauge what trends are emerging. Whether your research is formal or informal, it is also critical to look beyond your industry and follow technology, since increasingly that is where the most disruptive change is apt to come from. This chapter features articles that look at emerging trends and what your business should do to take advantage of them.

Mobile Disruption: Are You Ready to Buy with a #Hashtag?

. . .

Market forces, technology, and opportunity are converging on the mobile phone front and about to launch a huge disruptive force in commerce. While we have become accustomed to promotional and communication opportunities enabled by the Internet and social media, the distribution and pricing channel is about to heat up.

According to the recently released ***Comscore 2013 Digital Future in Focus Report***, smartphones in Canada now represent 62% of the market, up from 45% in 2012. This is significant in that we have now passed a tipping point where the majority of phone users are mobile Internet enabled. Couple this with Canadians spending on average 41 hours/month online, second only globally to Americans at 43 hours/month, and the stage has now been set for market forces and opportunity to collide with new disruptive offerings. Here are a couple of early examples.

Twitter has paired up with **American Express** to enable purchases to be completed with the use of a hashtag. Essentially once a consumer tweets a specific hashtag to the company requesting a purchase, the transaction would be completed once acknowledged by the company and then confirmed by the customer. Online shopping with all the extra hassle of security and transactions would be taken out of the system. It's a bold social media move by American Express and could indicate a disruptive shift in the way commerce will be conducted online in the future. It does however beg some privacy and ethical issues. Will people want their purchase history on Twitter? Does this make impulse shopping too easy? But beyond this dark side, there is certainly opportunity. Consumers will automatically be promoting brands to their followers while buying them. Suddenly there is equity to a company in how many followers a purchaser has, and that could lead to some interesting promotional offers to prospective customers. Privacy and ethics aside, there is a solid win-win formula potentially in there as marketers look for ways to leverage their brand within social channels. Read more here: http://www.forbes.com/sites/boninbough/2013/02/13/from-hashtag-to-purchase-twitters-newest-partnership-with-american-express/.

Apple has applied for a patent to get into the mobile micro-lending banking business via an innovative APP. They want to be able to turn iPhone users into potential ad-hoc cash dispensary locations. Essentially a consumer, who needs, say, $20 but is not close to a bank machine, could use their APP to find another iPhone user in proximity. They would receive the offer to lend that person $20 cash, which would then appear as an Apple credit on their iTunes account, plus a bonus transaction fee for having facilitated the exchange. This essentially makes everyday consumers into cash machines, while denying the banks their exorbitant service charges. You can bet that Apple plans to sell more than music in their iTunes commerce site, and I would think this signals a major move to tread into Amazon territory. It certainly would be more appealing to accumulate credits that could be used to purchase a broad range of things beyond just music. Read more here: http://techcrunch.com/2013/01/31/apple-patents-crowdsourced-peer-to-peer-mobile-banking-that-could-use-itunes-to-provide-cash-on-demand/.

Both of these examples work in a mobile-enabled consumer environment. Expect more of this type of innovative thinking from companies as technology, market forces, and opportunity disrupt traditional distribution channels.

8 Trends to Track in 2013

■ ■ ■

Christine Day, CEO of Lululemon, said something recently in conversation that has echoed with me for days. When asked how she keeps up with trends and ensures that her company is on the leading edge, she responded, 'I scan the environment reading magazines across many industries. I listen for what is next, not evidence of what has happened.'

How many gurus of trends and forecasting actually spout evidence, albeit applied to the future, of what has happened? And how many truly listen, often beyond their industry, for what is actually apt to be coming next? My guess is few.

In marketing, it is our job to know what is trending and to be alert enough to utilise that knowledge to our client's advantage.

Here is a mash-up from the BCAMA 2013 ad agency panel of observations gained from four presenters: Lance Saunders, VP managing director, DDB Canada; Ute Preusse, director, strategic planning, Cossette; Lance Neale, president, Station X; and Alvin Wasserman, president, Wasserman + Partners Advertising.

1. **Marketing is liquid.** Strategy, creativity, and execution are no longer written in stone. Good marketing is now interactive and utilises multiple media. That also means that traditional silos within agencies need to be liquid. Good ideas can come from anywhere.

2. **Brands need more full-frontal nudity.** Some brands have lost trust because they are *not* having conversations with their customers or are either continuing a traditional one-way push of their message or, worse, are pretending to

engage while spouting corporate-speak. The McDonald's 'Our food, your questions' campaign that encouraged customers to ask questions about food, nutrition, and photography used in advertising was cited as a good example of having an authentic conversation (http:// strategyonline.ca/2012/12/07/bravest-campaign-of-the-year-mcdonalds/). Bottom line: be transparent.

3. **Big data as a force of good, not evil.** Today companies have incredibly rich profiles of customers gained through online interaction and purchases. Using that data respectfully is key. Target got into trouble last year when their data tracking allowed them to profile customers' purchases to the point where they could actually predict if a customer was pregnant—thereby allowing them to engage on a personal level with offers appealing to an expectant mother. Trouble was, they sent a card to a teen girl's home, and her father intercepted questioning why it had been sent. Turns out Target know something Dad didn't. Ouch. That's just too personal (http://video. foxnews.com/v/1470704607001/target-knew-teen-was-pregnant-before-her-dad/). Google, on the other hand, was able to track flu outbreaks globally more accurately than the World Health Organization, simply by aggregating flu symptom search data by region. That's data being used for a force of good (http://technorati.com/technology/article/google-and-flu-tracking/).

4. **Everything has changed, and nothing has changed.** While technology has enabled so many things we could have only dreamed about decades ago, our fundamental values as humans have not changed. We still want to connect, share, and tell stories. We need to understand technology from the perspective of the *need* it fulfills.

5. **Retail is everywhere.** The ability to browse, shop, and buy is no longer grounded just in brick and mortar stores. Increasingly shopping will be facilitated by mobile devices, whether via online sites, apps, near field

communication, or creative applications in unexpected locations. Tesco installed a Homeplus virtual subway grocery store using photo images of products in South Korea. Users could purchase items via QR code scans from their mobile phones and have the items delivered to their home later that day (http://www.youtube.com/ watch?v=fGaVFRzTTP4).

6. **Emerging markets need to be on your radar.** The world has become more connected with brands going global for both opportunity and economy of scale. Time to learn Portuguese, Mandarin, and Panjabi as the emergence of the middle class continues in Brazil, China, and India.

7. **Going private in public.** As we become increasing more connected, the ability to unplug will become coveted. There are few places where urban dwellers can escape the temptation of checking in, posting, or responding to e-mail. With the exception of boarding a plane, or wandering off into the wilderness, the expectation of being 'on' has overwhelmed many. Kitkat in Amsterdam created Wi-Fi-free zones where benches had Wi-Fi jammers that blocked signals within a five-meter radius. Of course, the brand's tagline, 'Have a break, have a Kitkat' was well aligned with the effort (http://www.psfk. com/2013/01/kit-kat-wifi-free-zone.html). Norte Beer in Argentina offered an escape from photo indiscretions friends might capture at a nightclub and post to Facebook by inventing a 'Photoblocker' beer sleeve that detects a camera flash and emits a blast of light to make the photo contents indistinguishable (http://www.youtube.com/ watch?v=h5DJbKPS8d4). Both of these brands have successfully provided an escape from technology that hounds us, while positioning themselves as being on the consumer's side. Brilliant.

8. **Storytelling matters.** In the end, we are ruled by our hearts, not our heads. Use data to see what matters. Use technology to facilitate the connection. But remember that

it's the emotional connection and a basic human instinct to engage in and share stories that should drive campaigns. Brands with purpose that connect on an emotional level through storytelling will always rise above others.

And remember above all to listen for what is next, rather than seek evidence of what has happened.

Newspapers in 2013:
Not Dead, Just Different

. . .

As Mark Twain, noted American humorist declared in 1897, 'The reports of my death were greatly exaggerated.' The same could be said of print newspapers in 2013.

For much of the last century, print media organizations have staked their revenue success on the business of selling readers to advertisers. Circulation, readers per copy, and time spent with the publication has always been valued metrics. Demographic profiling that touted the spending power of readers was paraded before potential advertisers in the hope they would pay to have their message in front of this desirable group.

While many of those same publications have struggled with the shrinking advertising budget of clients, increased fragmentation of media, and the limits of the traditional one-way pull strategy of print ads, quietly a shift has been taking place.

Some early mavericks, brave enough to erect pay walls to access valuable content, are now seeing success. Believing that publishing on digital platforms doesn't mean you have to give away content, they have seen a steady increase in paid digital subscriptions. The *New York Times* announced recently that revenue from circulation exceeded revenue from advertising for the first time ever. Yes, you may want to read that again. That is a major shift, and the *Times* is likely an indication of an early tipping point (http://www.forbes.com/sites/zacks/2012/07/06/the-new-york-times-companys-rise-in-circulation-revenue/).

So how exactly did this happen when many media watchers were announcing the imminent death of newspapers and magazines? While we have generally become accustomed to information on the web being accessible for free, those pundits simply assumed the revenue model of the last century, essentially one honed post-industrial revolution would continue. Clearly a shift is taking place. And it just might be those tablets, heralded as the death nail of print, that actually become the savours, offering the platform to consume digital content on the go.

As print media companies struggle to adapt to the shifting revenue model, good content, as it always has, will sell.

Will We 'Graph Search' Instead of Google Search Soon?

■   ■   ■

Graph Search is a recently announced feature from Facebook and it's potentially a game changer in the search category currently dominated by Google. Getting people to utilise a new search tool within Facebook, is all aimed at keeping them within the platform, where the company can monetize their presence through targeted business advertising tied back to their search results. Facebook has compiled an incredible graph of aggregated data that, when combined with search, has the ability to deliver very personalized results based on your profile and your friend's experiences.

Suddenly a Google search could go from yielding 1,000 results for 'Best restaurant in Paris' to perhaps the top 5 as aggregated by recommendations based on your friend's personal experiences. That in itself is a pretty compelling draw, but if you add an additional layer of localized search enabled from mobile devices, where your physical proximity, is further aggregated with results to suggest the restaurant recommended by friends that is within walking distance at that very moment, that is, the holy grail. It is at that point that search not only becomes personal, but also location based, and in an increasingly mobile web environment, that is where all this is headed.

Local services, such as lawn care, roofing, decorating, plumbing, dry cleaning, or shoe repair, have not by and large, adopted Facebook pages and social media campaigns yet. However, search tied to location and aggregated data, including friend's recommendations, could dramatically change that. Want to find a roofing company that did work for your neighbours and was recommended by your friends? You'll be able to do that on Facebook. It makes a simple Google search for roofers and Vancouver, where I live, seem passé.

Google of course is the king of search. However, Facebook took a shot at them when they declared, 'The difference between web search and Graph Search is that Graph Search shows you the answer and not links to answers.'

One benefit to marketers is that Facebook will be conditioning its billions of users to search for what they're looking for, thus divulging intent, something they have never before been able to capture. The combination of social context (what your friends like) and intent (what you're looking to buy) will make it possible for advertisers to take Facebook's already amazing targeting to the next level.

I'm not sure where all this leaves Google+, but I would be very surprised to not see Google attempt to unite their own properties in a similar offering.

It's a high stakes game, and this major move by Facebook puts them squarely in Google's search territory. Currently Graph Search is in Beta form available to limited users. That won't last long.

Look out. This could get interesting.

Tracked, Targeted, and Tired: Consumers Go Private in Public as Leading Trend for 2013

. . .

We joke in our house that my husband is a digital dinosaur. He can text, but seldom does from his flip phone. He has no apps, isn't on Facebook, Twitter, or LinkedIn. He doesn't know what Pinterest is, doesn't blog, and only uses e-mail occasionally. Short of showing up in a Google search as having run a marathon, he has no digital footprint. Turns out, he might be a renaissance man after all, being ahead of an emerging trend for 2013 where consumers increasingly look to guard their information and digital persona.

After several years of displaying our lives publicly online, the holy grail may now be finding privacy on your own terms.

However, short of cutting yourself off from all social media and rejecting a smartphone, maintaining privacy has become a challenge. As companies change their settings and data use policies, finely tuned privacy walls can be destroyed with a few lines of code. As consumers, we are encouraged to read updated use statements, but we all know how easy it is to just press 'accept'.

And it's not just social media titans we now fear; it's our own 'friends' who share, post, tag, and comment. Just because something was done in public does not mean it should receive public promotion. From Facebook updates, to Tweets, and photos shared on Pinterest, we are a society verging on over-share. So what are creative consumers doing in response? They're creating Facebook identities with pseudonyms to guard against current and future employers. They're trimming friend lists back to actual friends rather than an extended ring of acquaintances. They're hosting 'photo free' and 'social sharing free' parties where smartphones are checked at the door. They're creating 'dark rooms' at social gatherings where no photos are allowed. They're making actual phone calls rather than producing something that can be digitally shared. If it sounds like a rejection of technology, think again. It's the use of technology but on your own terms.

There of course is marketing opportunity in this trend for the company or brand that recognizes it and taps into the sensibilities by 'playing on your team' to help protect that identity.

Norte Beer in Argentina invented a clever device called **Photoblocker**, which is basically a cooler sleeve for your beer at a nightclub. Photoblocker detects when a camera flash is about to capture a photo and emits a blast of light to make the photo contents indistinguishable, thereby protecting whatever indiscretions about to be captured. The brainchild of **Del Campo Nazca Saatchi & Saatchi**, Buenos Aires, one could argue the morality of such a device. But you can't argue how it puts Norte Beer on the consumer's side of the battle for social media privacy. See video of Photoblocker in action here: http://www.youtube.com/watch?v=h5DJbKPS8d4.

In yet another beer company application in Argentina (please reserve judgement on the need for such a device in this country), **Andes Beer** invented a soundproof **Teletransporter**, allowing guys to place calls from a soundproof booth to their girlfriends while at a nightclub, appearing to be somewhere else. See video here: https://www.youtube.com/watch?v=iKDgYKSEN6M.

While these two examples obviously target a young male demographic, they represent examples of creativity in action that is right on trend.

Finding ways to be private in public is just one of ten highlighted trends in the **JWT Top Trends for 2013 report**. The report is an annual forecast of key trends that will significantly impact consumer behaviour for the near future. Check out a short video summarizing the trends here: http://www.youtube.com/watch?v=bCDs7zQELpM.

JWT invests a tremendous amount in researching social and cultural trends, which they release in their annual study. Link here to buy the full 2013 report: http://www.jwtintelligence.com/shop/10-trends-for-2013/.

The Little Sign That Could

. . .

Poised below a former iconic sign landmarking HMV's presence at Burrand and Robson in Vancouver is a little iPod sign. Appearing without threat, but determination like the children's tale of the little red engine that could, it in fact did. Metaphorically, it toppled an iconic brand from its throne.

Photo: Mary Charleson

HMV closed some months ago and until recently sat vacant waiting new tenants willing to pay high rent for a prime location. HMV was a victim in the end of changing technologies and distribution of its product. The fact that that the iPod was the product that introduced music digitization and sharing and was ultimately the downfall of music sellers like HMV was poignant. Even more poignant since the iPod sign was the only thing left hanging in the store. The iPad has recently disrupted another industry as well.

I was lamenting the closure of one of my favourite bookstores, Book Warehouse, in Vancouver recently. Although not encumbered by debt, overexpansion, or an invisible cash flow, the owner was selling off the stock from multiple locations and calling it quits. It would seem that the forces of increased online competition, a squeeze on margins, the emergence of e-books and readers, and a publishing industry reeling with the forces of technology and trying to redefine itself had taken its toll. That and the fact that the founders, all ready to retire, were looking to sell their business at a time of great turmoil in the publishing and book industry.

But as the owner, an accomplished professional musician, said with a smile on his face the day I talked to him moving fixtures out of the Lonsdale location and packing up what was left of inventory to be donated to a first nations library, 'The book business fed my music habit for over thirty years. I'm happy!' Admittedly, it was a pretty positive spin on what could only be lamented as a huge shame in the face of changing technologies. A shame because there will be five less bookstores to browse in Vancouver. And a shame because, along with all the people who those stores have employed, the owners will not realize any equity from pouring over thirty years of time into the business.

Book Warehouse fended off the onslaught of big box bookstores in the '90s when many independents failed. It withstood the ongoing price competition from online retailers such as Amazon. They had carved out a niche based on selling books bought back from publishers at huge discounts and then selling at bargain prices, while still achieving higher margins than their competitors. They were able to sell best sellers at huge discounts and still make money unlike most competitors because their entire business model was based on low costs and no leverage. It worked for many years because it was not easily copied.

The lesson learned through these two examples? While you can have a defined market niche, a great product or service, and be at the top of your game, the external forces of technology and changing consumer habits can put it all into question. In the end, every business must monitor and adapt to change.

Is Google+ the New Facebook, Twitter, and LinkedIn Combined?

. . .

Many business leaders I speak to greet the opportunity to create and manage another social media identity with the same anticipation as a root canal. They question the necessity of it and the time required.

I've been watching with great interest the growth of **Google+**. At 90 million users (January 2012), they are still a far cry from **Facebook**'s 800 million users. Arguably with Facebook's IPO announcement recently, that company has been garnering all the press. However, the power behind Google's online clout and ownership of search can't be denied. That and their ownership of Android with a major stake in the mobile market, along with the Google wallet mobile payment system recently launched in the US, makes them, in my mind, a bigger player. Oh yes, and they own that little station called **YouTube**. There is a major mud-slinging match being waged between these two titans that have the ability to aggregate human behaviour on the web. They want to use that data to offer a predictive user experience and, of course, sell micro-targeted advertising content.

Commercialism aside, I think to ignore the potential benefits to a business that actively participates in content sharing on these networks is to do so at your own peril. Increasingly having a **Google+** or **Facebook** presence will be as important, if not more important, than having your own website, because that content will be tied to social media rankings and ratings, mobile search, and customer feedback in addition to what you want to tell people about yourself. Consider how after spending $3.5 million for their **2012 Super Bowl spot 'Seduction'**, Fiat simply directed viewers to their **Facebook Fiat 500 Abarth** page rather than their website. They recognized their target was likely to be watching and browsing on mobile devices throughout the game. Viewers could immediately interact with others about the spot, and of course the car. In a world where 54% of customers trust comments by friends, 35% trust comments by strangers, and 47% say even a single negative review can impact their potential purchase, which becomes important (**TNS Global Digital Media study**).

I have to say, that in the short time since joining **Google+**, I have been able to connect with some brilliant minds in my industry and share valuable content. I have tended to use **Facebook** for family and friends primarily, while balancing some business use with closer connections and clients. I tend to use **Twitter** as a follower to gain insights, while pushing out what I think is important from a marketing perspective only when I can actually be insightful. I've reserved **LinkedIn** for a professional circle of business contacts, aiming to acquire quality over quantity. Together, these social media tools are a potent and powerful mix for networking, connecting, and professional positioning. My initial experiences with Google+ have enabled me to combine the best of all the other networks combined. I am able to create circles and manage who receives my posts and shared content. Facebook has also made changes recently to make groups easier, but I find the posting options in Google+ easier, since I can choose multiple groups and different combinations, depending on the content I am posting. With Google+, I am able to 'follow' the public posts of leaders and influencers just like Twitter, which Facebook does not allow. And because the interface is built on circles of influence, there is an earned reciprocity based on professional reputation and value of content shared that gives it additional value over LinkedIn. Your digital footprint is aggregated in one place that connects out to everything else you have on the web, which is used by Google to further boost your search engine results. Plus Google+ has some very cool features such as 'meet up', which allows users to video chat. I participated in the Columbia School of Journalism's Social

Media Weekend global meetup recently. This feature puts a whole new spin on possibilities for conferences, education applications, business meetings, and consumer focus groups. Of course, Google+ will only be as powerful as the uptake of users that get on board, and at this stage, that is its limiting factor. But it is a tool that holds promise in the face of Facebook's dominance.

In the end, I admit to continuing my double dating efforts between Facebook and Google+ as well as maintaining Twitter and LinkedIn. I'm just not sure where all this might be going, so I'm not ready to make a full commitment to one over the other. I encourage you to check out the benefits of Google+ for yourself and let me know what you think.

Get ready for huge battles to be waged over the access to human behaviour data on the web. And expect the friction between personal privacy and the freedom of information from legislation to be at the heart of it!

Is Google Destroying Users' Faith in Them as a Fair and Unbiased Source of Information?

■ ■ ■

Google appears to be preferentially placing its own results in their new Google Plus Your World approach. Some consumers have taken notice of the changes in search rankings recently. This perceived influence and public silence on the changes they have made harkens back to the *big brother* days of George Orwell's *1984*. Perhaps that's being a little extreme, but paired with the recent uproar over SOPA in the US, there is definitely a heightened awareness over control of content, and particular the feeling that the Internet should be free of bias and control.

Over time this could put them squarely in a public relations crisis, or worse, destroy the brand perception of Google as 'owning search'. That is their unique selling proposition in the market. They need to guard that position carefully.

This could be dangerous territory. Back in the dark ages, the '80s, when I worked in print media at the *Georgia Straight* in Vancouver, we realized the line between advertisers and editorial is one to be respected. If you start to play with advertising influence, your readers lose respect for the editorial authenticity. This is really the same fundamental issue 2012 style. If influence emerges that impacts the value of search results, and that influence is there because they use your products (Google+), you lose respect of users.

I do however see an interesting and appealing business model in combining a search offering that considers your circles of interest and influence. Maybe Google needs to introduce a tab that allows both options. Either way, they should come clean with what they are doing and allow transparency so the benefits can be appreciated. It's pretty obvious how search results are different now depending on if you are logged into Google or not.

Are You Willing To Bet Against Google?

. . .

The cover of *Fast Company* magazine recently caught my eye. A photo of Larry Page, CEO of Google, was plastered on the front, with the heading, '**Look out Apple, Facebook & Amazon—Why Google will win**'. The cover was a plug for an article inside called 'The Great Tech War of 2012' (http://www.fastcompany.com/magazine/160/tech-wars-2012-amazon-apple-google-facebook).

I pulled it off the shelf. That's when things got interesting.

Behind it was a red-coloured version of the same magazine, but with Steve Jobs's face on the cover and a headline, 'Why Apple Will Win'. A little more rummaging led me to find a total of four versions of the same November 2011 issue, a clever ploy to promote the article. The other versions exclaimed why Facebook or Amazon would win.

The quandary then became, 'Which cover to purchase?'

Photo: Mary Charleson

All four companies have disrupted various industries. In a period of less than five years, they have changed the entertainment, music, publishing, and media industries. They had also disrupted gaming, retail, mobile, communications, and advertising. Payment systems and cloud computing are on their radar.

Initially I gravitated towards the **Apple** cover, but Steve Jobs's prominent photo started looking like a question mark to me with his recent death and the uncertainty of continued innovation.

Amazon is brazen and innovative, but anchored to the end of the commerce funnel. Not a bad place to be, but limited. I figured it would come down to who controlled insights on people and information.

Facebook arguably knows more about our behaviours than we do ourselves, and they have the muscle to leverage that knowledge. But in the end, I chose the **Google** cover. Why?

Google owns search. When we are searching, we are seeking. And seeking is the beginning of every desire. Now that they have entered the foray of social media with Google+, I believe they will ultimately hold the trump card. They can access our profile and the gateway to our desired transactions. They will have the ability to utilise our preferences and the influence of our social circle to control our individual search results. Suddenly, it's not just a Google search, it's 'Knowing you, I would suggest,' and that becomes extremely powerful. Powerful ultimately, since marketers will pay attention to it.

My own personal example: I received an invitation to join **Google+** from a colleague. I created a quick account, putting minimal content on it. Doing a search a week later, to my horror, the Google+ link had outranked my company website www.charleson.ca and my blog www.fiveminutemarketing.com each with a long history, massive content, and multiple links on the web. I have since made the account more robust and now monitor search ranks. Subsequently Google appears to have changed search to favour content producers. but here are my takeaways:

1. **Google+ is in search results like never before.** A Google+ profile outranks other content. You may feel that using their clout to adjust rankings in their favour is unfair, but it's a compelling reason to claim a Google+ profile.
2. **You will want to create large circles. Everything you share on Google+ will be ranked higher, and if you have more people in your circles, it will be ranked higher still.** Because Google now appears to favour quality content, you can use that to position yourself. You would be foolish to not share everything through Google+ to boost your search rankings.
3. **Their recent 'Google Search Plus Your World' introduced the influence of your social circle into search results.** Logged-in users receive socially shared content from their circles in the results—essentially tying social media into search results. Although the bias appears to diminish when logged out, Google+ linked content still rises in the search rankings. Facebook's power is its 800 million users. Google+ with a current 90 million users may

seem small by comparison. However, when you combine the billions of people doing billions of searches daily on Google, the user group and influence is exponential.

Is Google+ just another social media tool to maintain? Yes, but the choice not to participate could have far-reaching implications on your business. In the end, I bought the Larry Page cover of *Fast Company* because I am not willing to bet against Google. Are you? Want to connect on Google+? http://bit.ly/xcTbco

The Sheconomy

■ ■ ■

Recently marketers have coined a new term, as they are wont to do, called the 'Sheconomy'. Roughly translated, this refers to the economic influence of women.

Canadian Labour Market statistics point to the fact that the recent recession has favoured the sheconomy, where men experienced steeper and more prolonged employment declines than women did. Much of this is related to the decline in manufacturing and construction, where men held a large majority of jobs. Conversely, the service sector, often dominated by women, has experienced growth. This same pattern played out during the recessions of the 1980s and 1990s as well. As a result, employment has grown more rapidly among women than among men during the last three decades. Jobs in the new knowledge-based economy we are told will demand people skills, emotional intelligence, team effort, and multitasking, skills that tend to favour the female playbook. These facts, while interesting, are only part of the picture.

Over at Statistics Canada, we find proof that the gals are eclipsing the guys on the education front. Currently 61% of all university graduates are women, and that is up from 56% in 1992. While we can scratch our heads about a troubled system that now seems to leave our boys behind, it signals a major shift for the upcoming decades of consumers. Higher education equals higher income. There will be power in that purse.

A recent Pew study of thirty—to forty-four-year-olds showed that when a husband is the primary or sole breadwinner, household spending decisions are divided roughly equally. He makes about a third of them, she makes a third, and they make a third jointly. But in the 22% of households studied in which the wife earned more, she made more than twice as many decisions as her husband about where the money would go. The more money women earn, the exponentially more money they manage.

Now before this article comes off as a Gloria Steinem lecture on the power of women, I simply want to state that these shifts will have a profound impact on your marketing efforts in the coming decades. This is not about marketing to women. It's about marketing well, recognizing that these subtle shifts have handed women significant influence on many purchases.

How might that affect your marketing?

1. **Consider the increasing power of social networks.**
   There are over 500 million people on Facebook. Close to 60% of them are women, and women are the most active group in terms of sharing content. YouTube streams 1.2 billion views per day. These tools alone under the tender care of millions of self-appointed editorial writers and videographers could fame or shame a brand in days. Given the tendency of women to befriend other women, share information, chat, and stay connected, it comes as no surprise that she has taken to social networks so naturally. Are you the person at the party working the room and bragging about your accomplishments, or are you the one engaging conversation, asking questions, and sharing information? In the cocktail party that is social networks, she likes the latter.

2. **Consider the research phase involved in a purchase.**
   While this is particularly important for higher-priced items such as cars, appliances, holidays, and houses, it holds true for 85% of all purchases where research suggests women have significant influence. While both genders conduct research, women are much more apt to read online reviews and verify information. Women are also more likely to seek out the opinion of others. While guys look for a

good solution through a methodical process of collecting information, identifying priorities, and eliminating quickly options that don't meet their criteria, women look for the best solution by researching and adding information until all options are exhausted. Her process is often less direct and takes more time. From a marketing perspective, understanding the importance of the research phase for women is key. Respecting her need to become informed and helping her collect information are critical. Are your salespeople trained to do that? Is your website set up to help with this? Do you engage social media with this goal in mind?

While these points may help you capture more female decision makers in the sheconomy, these efforts are ultimately aimed at all customers. That's just good marketing.

Will the Tablet Change Your Business?

• • •

This article originally appeared in late 2010, and some of the questions that it addresses now seem redundant. It would appear that in the ensuing three years, the tablet has indeed become a necessity for many. What I think is important to reflect on now is how quickly this change took place and the importance of having your trend-spotting radar poised as you look into the future.

Take one tablet daily and call your doctor if your condition doesn't improve. That's the advice we're accustomed to receiving when taking medication. But it would seem that both consumers and businesses are in a quest for help with what ails them these days, judging by the uptake of the tablet—also known as the Apple iPad, Blackberry Playbook, HP Slate, and the Google Android Tablet.

What's with the sudden revolution and the apparent need for a hybrid between your smartphone and your laptop? Lots, it would seem. This isn't a tech column, so I'm not going to go into comparing features and benefits, but let's assume for the time being that this is not a fad. It's a trend. Consider:

- Apple's iPad sales hit 2 million in 59 days after the April release in Canada. Sales are expected to hit 9.7 million worldwide for 2010.
- HP and Google jump on board the tablet bandwagon in summer 2010. Todd Bradley, HP's executive vice president for Personal Systems Group, estimates tablets will become a $40 billion market over the next few years.

- RIM, the maker of Blackberry, announces the Playbook in fall 2010, with a market launch in early 2011.

Clearly tablets are the new frontier. All the major players are lining up to battle for market share.

This could be a game-changing trend. And trends are critically different than fads when it comes to evaluating the impact on your marketing strategy. So what does this all mean to you?

I'd suggest you step back from the day-to-day busy work and consider possible impacts on your business. Take the 10,000-meter view if you will. Think big picture and think what this looks like five years from now. Brainstorm some possible effects on your business. Look at the threats as well as the opportunities. Now consider what you should be doing today to mitigate those threats or take advantage of those opportunities.

Let's look at an example to get you considering the process.

Suppose you are a book retailer or are in the publishing industry. You've barely recovered from the consolidation of the industry with big box retail, the increasing competitiveness from online retailers, and now e-books are on the horizon. In July, Amazon sold 180 e-books for every 100 hardcover books. They of course push their own reader, the Kindle, but sell books that can be read on any tablet device. Chapters/Indigo have a robust offering of online e-books and their own competitively priced reader, the Kobo. There's also the Sony Reader and the Barnes & Noble Nook. Supported by a wide variety of readers and tablets, electronic books are going mainstream.

This trend will be further fuelled by the explosive growth and run for market share in the tablet market led by Apple's iPad. Expect the e-book to be under the Christmas tree this year. At first blanch, it's not hard to see the threat if you're in the business of selling tangible books. How do you position and price your offerings? Will this change your target market and segmentation? Are there new niche opportunities? How might the inevitable consolidation of the publishing industry and entrance of new 'entertainment company' publishers affect your future? The e-book is bound to attract a more tech-savvy publishing model that supports video and interactive content in addition to the written word. Where might the opportunities lie in that?

Prior to the launch of the iPad, Steve Jobs is rumoured to have said, 'This is the most important thing I've ever done.' Upon its launch, Disney CEP Bob Iger called it 'a game changer'. Hyperbole or fact? Only time will tell. But if history repeats itself, the iPad could do to the book industry what the iPod did to the music industry. The product, distribution system, pricing, and promotion all changed. Industry titans were toppled or became shadows of their former self and new players emerged.

The lesson here? No industry will be left untouched by the potential impact of the tablet. Time to get out your crystal ball so you can mitigate those threats and be the first to jump at the new opportunities.

The 35-Divide

■ ■ ■

In 1964, a student at the University of California-Berkeley named Jack Weinberg coined the immortal phrase, 'Don't trust anyone over thirty.' When he invoked that sentiment in 1964, Mr. Weinberg was a civil rights activist frustrated by bureaucratic inaction. Yet today, curiously that line still exists, in particular with respect to technology. I call it the *35-divide*.

My company recently completed a study on media use habits with **TNS Canadian Facts**. Results were based on 1,017 responses from across Canada. We looked at where the primary sources of news and information were, as well as measuring the growth of various online digital activities. Although there were exceptions in many areas, there was a definite line in the sand at 35 years. Those under 35 have different media habits from those over 35. We also busted some myths around just how important (or not) some digital media vehicles actually are. The Coles notes? Before abandoning traditional media for the digital bandwagon, consider your target group carefully.

What is your primary source of news and information?

	Overall	18-24yrs	25-34yrs	35-49yrs	50-64yrs
TV	42%	22%	35%	40%	49%
Newspaper	20%	22%	12%	17%	23%
Online news sites	18%	30%	31%	23%	8%
Radio	16%	7%	13%	19%	18%
Social networks	1%	10%	0.8%	0.4%	0

What is your secondary source of news and information?

	Overall	18-24yrs	25-34yrs	35-49yrs	50-64yrs
TV	27%	15%	36%	24%	26%
Newspaper	27%	28%	16%	26%	34%
Radio	19%	7%	8%	24%	23%
Online news sites	17%	22%	28%	18%	11%
Social networks	2%	4%	2%	2%	1%

TV ranked highest overall as both a primary and secondary source followed by newspapers. Online news sites were third highest, followed by radio as a primary source. The strength of online news sites was considerable for those 18-34 years. The question then becomes, which side of the sandy line does your primary target fall? If it falls under 35 years, online is your growth area, but TV and newspapers are still a very viable vehicle. If it falls over 35 years, online has its merits, but TV, newspapers, and radio are still your best primary vehicle.

Are you all a twitter about Twitter? Consider the 35-divide again and your primary target audience. We asked respondents if they were spending more, the same, or less time than a year ago microblogging with Twitter. Overall 2% were spending more time, 6% the same, and 13% were spending less time. Thirty-three per cent of those 18-34 years and 37% of those 25-34 years used Twitter. Contrast this to 19% of 35-49 years and 16% of 50-64 years who tweet. The use of Twitter with its limit of 140 characters clearly favours mobile devices, and it appears to be a tool dominated by young urban audiences in our research. The question then becomes, is that your audience?

Are you busting your butt to post to your blog regularly? Consider this fact: 73% of Canadians don't blog. Those that do are spending less time on it than a year ago. However, for the 27% of the population who do, the largest number is found under 35 years. Sixty-three per cent of those 18-24 years and 39% of those 25-34 years engage in this activity. 'There is a perception that blogging and using Twitter are bigger than they actually are,' notes **Raymond Gee, senior researcher, TNS Canadian Facts.**

Text messaging has grown, but is still a technology divided by age. While 53% of Canadians overall are sending text messages, 85% of 18-24 years and 80% of 25-34 years are doing it.

The trend towards smartphones, such as the iPhone and Blackberry, has growing tremendously. In fact, a recent **Deloitte** study estimates that smartphones will outnumber computers in the US by the first half of 2010. So just who is accessing information and news on their mobile device? Overall 40% of Canadians engage in this activity. But here again the 35-divide plays out. Seventy per cent of 18-24 years and 57% of 25-34 years are doing it. Instinctively I would have thought more professionals, and a greater representation of those over 35 years, would be relying on their device for news information. The takeaway here? Digital tools offer tremendous opportunity, but the euphoria over them shouldn't cloud the assessment of whether they are the right choice to reach your target group.

2010 Predictions for Marketing: A Reflection on What Has Changed, or Not!

. . .

As noted in the headline, this piece was originally written in early 2010. Now some three years later, it is interesting to reflect on what has actually happened and what trends will continue to play forward. Curiously, much that was predicted has transpired, or is in the course doing so.

It's a New Year and time to break out the crystal ball for a look at what to expect from the world of marketing. I believe 2010 will be a year of tremendous change. A few predictions:

1. **Digital will continue grow.** It hardly seems to be going out on a limb to forecast that one; however, the degree to which it will take over our lives will be considerable. Marketing is a lagging indicator. Forrester Research estimates our TV viewing at 35% of entertainment time. Currently 31% of marketing budgets are spent on TV. While 34% of time is spent on the Internet, only 12% of advertising is allocated there. Expect that gap to continue to close in 2010 as marketing dollars follow where consumers are increasingly spending their time. This is likely to manifest through increasing use of social networks and interactive web-based content being included in marketing strategies. As consumers are more able to influence brands in the digital space, it will become even more important to focus on the basics of good marketing:

appeal to a market segment, have a distinct advantage, innovate and stay ahead of competition, and practice unbelievably good customer service.

2. **Mobile will explode.** Currently 80% of phones in North America are used for voice only. The phone is being used as a phone. It's a novel concept. Although it may seem everyone around you is a slave to their Blackberry, in reality, market penetration for smartphones and data plans has a way to go to reach full potential. However, **Deloitte and Touche** estimate that smartphones will outnumber computers in the US by the first half of 2010. As they become commonplace, we will see a shift of marketing strategy and budgets towards this medium. Count on Google to figure prominently. With their Android mobile operating system, a new phone being sold direct to consumers and a near monopoly as content aggregator and advertising server, Google will be a game changer.

3. **Print will evolve.** Print's fundamental challenges really don't revolved around print itself. Digital media has been changing the game from the outside. We can expect a few titans to become shadows of their former self as this medium responds to market pressures. Those who provide commodity content, such as breaking news and non-exclusive stories, will struggle. Those who have differentiating content, such as critical analysis, exclusive stories, and a targeted product for a particular market niche will do just fine. 2010 may mark the year where print publishers will try to garner revenue from online ads plus paid content. In a world where a lot of good stuff is free, this will be a challenge. The *Wall Street Journal* has succeeded in getting readers to pay for content. So has the *Harvard Business Review*. Both dominate a niche market and provide exclusive stories. However, consumers have already demonstrated that they will pay for content and apps on cell phones. Electronic editions tailored for display on

smartphones might be an intriguing avenue for publishers to consider.

4. **Advertising agencies will struggle to monetize the new digital media model.** Digital media has caused marketing to evolve from one-way communication to where consumers now take part in blogs and social networks and influence the brand on a consumer-to-consumer level. Advertisers no longer control the message to the extent that they once did. Add compensation to the mix. Existing pricing models, based on front-end costs and paid media are still dominant, but with social media and other forms of earned media increasingly playing a pivotal role, ad agencies will need to reconsider how to price their services and restructure exactly where they will fit in as clients demand social media solutions and digital strategies. Expect some major shifts in this business model.

5. **TV will increasingly become a precision niche-marketing tool rather than a blunt instrument of mass media.** Although TV has traditionally reached the masses, with the exception of major sporting event coverage, or a worldwide news event, it just doesn't garner the mass audience it used to. And in 2010, we'll accept that and begin to use it to our advantage. As smaller groups watch increasingly niche programming, advertisers will be able to take advantage of commercials designed for specific episodes or a distinct group of viewers. Increasingly advertisers will be shaping content to the audience and then driving viewers online.

Mobile Media—the New Frontier

■ ■ ■

In January 2012, I first wrote about the power of WOM—word of mouth, mouse, and mobile—and how all three were working in concert influence consumer persuasion, as increasingly marketers are dealing with the opportunities of interaction, not just a one-way push of their message. A sea of e-mails later, and numerous comments following talks I have done on this topic, I've decided to look a little deeper into the last area, mobile, and how it is going to rock the ground we marketers walk on.

The federal government has allowed **Globalive Wireless** to become Canada's newest cell phone company. Significant in that this move breaks from the previous ruling to prohibit foreign-owned companies from setting up shop here. Previously **Telus**, **Rogers**, and **Bell** had it pretty much sewn up. Clearly, this signals a move to increased competition. Expect more. Apple recently forced the hand of Rogers, previously its exclusive distributor. Now the **Apple** iPhone is available on Telus and Bell networks. Could it be that these industry players expect a major battle in the coming year? You betcha.

A recent **Deloitte and Touche** survey reports that smartphones will outnumber computers in the US by the first half of 2010. That is a significant development. Marketing is a lagging indicator, following where consumers spend their time. We know they are increasingly spending it with digital media. And mobile media is about to take over. Very soon mobile will be the primary way consumers access and interact with the web. This, folks, is the new frontier.

Google, whose fortunes come from advertising, has plans to launch their own phone, bypassing wireless carriers and selling directly to consumers. You can bet they intend to reap ad dollars from mobile. **EMarketer.com** predicts online advertising revenue will grow 6% next year, compared to 40% for mobile. By controlling the handset, applications, and the user experience, Google could control their own mobile destiny. Currently handset makers and telecom carriers have the most say in the user experience, and carriers subsidize handsets in order to harvest the proceeds of a long-term data plan contract.

So what if Google leaned on advertising to recoup its handset development costs in order to control the end user application experience? What if under this disruptive model Google gave away voice, data, and text services in order to capture and monetize the resulting traffic?

This model would lead to price compression in exchange for locked-in connectivity that guarantees sizable audiences for advertisers. Smartphones and data plans would simply become a commodity, subject to price wars. Sitting on top, as a content aggregator, would be Google.

Of course this direct distribution model is similar to the one that Apple initially took with iPhone, and it wasn't until they sold handsets subsidized through carriers that they achieved market penetration. The same could hold true for Google.

We can say with some certainty that with increased competition and potentially disruptive distribution models, the mobile space is about to get very interesting. Soon the only phone available will be the smartphone, and in increasing numbers, consumers will have it in their pocket or bag and be able to access it 24/7. That is going to fundamentally change the way we connect with them. Be it pushed-out messages, ambient awareness tied to your location, or offers based on known interests, mobile has the ability to connect one on one at a personal level. Applications that seamlessly integrate information from **Facebook**, **Twitter**, **Flickr**, and **YouTube** accounts into you address book will make social networking a breeze. Suddenly 'word of mobile' will be just as important as word of mouth and word of mouse for getting others to spread your message.

What's the takeaway here? Marketers need a mobile strategy. Where the investment should be is on the development of content that provokes interaction with customers causing them to willingly spread your message. But remember, you need to be good if you want positive talk. You are no longer fully in control of your message, and that's a major shift. Advertising agencies are still struggling with how to monetize this model. This is indeed interesting territory.

Renegade and Everyman Brands on the Rise

∎ ∎ ∎

Meet the *renegade* and the *everyman*. The renegade is a challenger. He does things differently. Frequently seen as the underdog initially, he can often grow to become quite powerful. Never one to shy away from a dust-up, he is at his best when matched with a challenger, knowing he has identified an underserved populist niche.

The everyman is synonymous with the common masses. He is likeable, fun loving, and down to earth. Although he started out small, and may have grown to considerable stature, an air of modesty prevails. The everyman wears a ball cap and drinks coffee with his buddies. The renegade figures out how to serve them coffee in a new and revolutionary way.

The renegade and the everyman are brand positions that hold much promise these days. Why? Recent outrage over CEOs petitioning for bailouts and investment companies accepting bonuses in the wake of mismanagement has made for a belligerent consumer sentiment towards big business. Being seen as common folk has never been more popular. And if you can play David while filling a market niche and take a run at a Goliath-style company who may have lost that common touch, all the better in the eye of today's consumer.

Renegades are on the rise, and in many categories. Education had the University of Waterloo back in the 1980s, when they revolutionized universities with their co-op work/study program. Ivy League institutions scoffed at the time, but no longer. Waterloo-based Research in Motion, the designer of Blackberry, was a prodigy of this approach. University Canada West offers BCom and MBA students smaller classes, the ability to finish faster, and save a significant amount of money. Dismissed initially by bigger institutions, they are filling a growing niche. WestJet's biggest feat, besides streamlining an incredibly efficient cost model, was the fact that they *were not* Air Canada. A likeable renegade is hard to resist. Mr. Lube revolutionized the car care market. By keying in on everything that the dealer experience was not, they showed that fast, efficient, inexpensive, and convenient service was possible. And locally based credit union Vancity effectively challenged the traditional position of banks by profit sharing with their customers and supporting community ventures. However, their renegade spirit may have been tarnished of late with the decision to raise line of credit rates, seen by many to be non-Vancity-like, which was later retracted after media and member uproar. Likewise the decision to part with the insurance arm of the company, and to now serve members through the Co-operators, an Ontario-based company, was seen as a big-bank-like move, not typical of the renegade they thought they knew. A renegade can be a hard position to maintain with company growth or market force changes.

Everyman brands now have the power to connect more than ever before. The challenge for everyman brands is to maintain the position as they grow. Easily achieved in business infancy, it can be hard to maintain a common touch with growth. Tim Hortons is an everyman brand. Offering a basic consumable in big cities and small towns across the country, they *are not* Starbucks, a decidedly urban brand, and proud of it. They support their local communities, offer a meeting place for people to connect, and they are with Canadians in hand as they go about everyday activities, such as taking kids to soccer or hockey practice.

Motel 6 is another everyman brand. With their awe-shucks radio ad narrator, Tom Bodett, charming audiences with humorous commentary, down-home fiddle music in the background, and a final gesture, 'We'll leave the light on for you,' they have effectively shown that Joe Average can have some luxury without too much flash and can save money. In fact, they're a bit of an everyman *and* a renegade wrapped into one.

Although it would be foolish to abandon a current marketing position for the latest flavour of the month, you should consider how elements of the *everyman* or *renegade* spirit can be incorporated in your efforts. Brands who are not aligned in some way with these values right now will struggle.

Branded Video Search Links Integrate Digital and Traditional Media

• • •

Video is more powerful than words on the page. That's what Yahoo! is counting on with its recent launch of embedding purchased images and video space within search results. The new offering is called *Rich Ads in Search*.

Brands and agencies, including Pepsi, Home Depot, Victoria's Secret, and Pedigree, have tested new rich media search ads on Yahoo! in the US; a UK roll-out is now in the works. There's no word on Canada, but expect an expansion in the future. This is definitely an approach to watch.

Traditional search advertising typically shows only text advertising and links. Along with sponsored results, the Yahoo! offering enables brands to put promotional videos in top searches. Victoria's Secret and Pedigree dog food have added video to their campaigns so far. When you search phrases for either of these companies, they come out top of the list with a video link icon that's pretty hard to resist for the YouTube generation. The approach is based on 'opt in' rather than an obtrusive pop-up ad or easy-to-ignore static banner, so audiences are much more apt to be receptive to the message. Plus as the recession has deepened, many advertisers have shifted money to search, which gives them direct, measurable results. Return on investment (ROI) has increasingly become the top prize.

In the US, participating advertisers' click-through rates rose by as much as 25% during trials, while brand exposure also increased.

The program has now expanded beyond the initial pilot done in February and will be rolled out internationally.

Yahoo! will be charging a monthly fee for its *Rich Ads in Search*, though the company has said it might revert to the auction-based pricing model in the future.

Rival Google has also been trialing video search listings in the US. Although Yahoo! has introduced this search feature, it might be the Google version that causes it to take off. Google sites led the market in December with 63% of the searches conducted. Yahoo! gained some ground with a 21% market share, a 0.5% increase at Google's expense. Microsoft has repeatedly expressed interest in purchasing Yahoo!'s search business, so you can hedge your bets that this approach will likely grow in the future.

So why do I think this is an important trend? Two reasons:

1. **With our recession economy, people are doing more online research before making purchase decisions now than a year ago.** Recent research by Miller Zell Inc. in the US reveals that 44% of all respondents were doing more online research than they were a year ago. The trend is likely to be similar in Canada. More online searches will mean it is becoming increasingly important to rank at the top of search listings with a compelling reason to click on the link.

2. **While TV viewing is becoming increasingly fragmented with multiple stations, time shifting of viewing, and commercial skipping, the traditional 30-second spot is getting lost in the shuffle.** The Bureau of Broadcast Measurement (BBM) pegs overall household penetration of DVRs in Canada, those machines that allow commercials to be skipped, at 12-14%. The loss of TV viewing also seems to be at the expense of time spent online. Recent research by TNS Canadian Facts found that 22% of people were watching less TV than a year ago, but their online activities such as social networking, sending e-mails, and viewing of websites had increased

during that time. Watching videos on YouTube has become increasingly popular and this new offering to embed video in the search engine result feeds the shift in use patterns we have observed, particularly with younger audiences.

Of course if embedded video becomes too popular, content will fail to stand out on a page filled with these links. However, as a tool to help integrate digital and online media, it's right on target for the times. Stay tuned, and don't touch that dial—I mean, mouse!

word of
**M UTH
M USE &
M BILE**
CHAPTER 3

Branding Your Businesses, Your Ideas, or Your Products

■   ■   ■

Branding is at the very root of good marketing. On the outside, your brand is a combination of elements that identify you and distinguish you from competitors. But on the inside, great branding starts with having an element of storytelling and a distinct competitive advantage, which is rewarded with an emotional connection formed with the customer. This chapter looks at brands that have successfully mastered all three elements of storytelling, competitive advantage, and emotion.

The Beardo and the Beermo: Social Media Success from Canada, eh?

. . .

Some of us are counting down the days until the end of November when the faces of Movember men are replaced by the clean-shaven. For those lamenting the passing of this hairy month, you may find solstice in the Canadian-made Beardo or Beermo courtesy of http://www.beardowear.ca/.

Photo: Used with permission by Jeff Phillips, Beardowear

Photo: Used with permission by Jeff Phillips, Beardowear

The brainchild of Jeff Phillips, a snowboarder who found his face frozen atop Whistler Mountain, this quirky product line has taken off, mostly courtesy of the power of social media, which then fuelled traditional media, and then was funneled back to social to keep the interest embers stoked and burning. I stumbled upon it initially while peering over the shoulder of my fourteen-year-old son's Facebook page. I'm not sure if he was feeling prematurely follicularly challenged, or simply helping to further fuel the word of mouth, mouse, and mobile, but currently the Beardowear Facebook page sits at 83,846 likes and 7,426 talking about this. Have a look: http://www.facebook.com/beardowear.

There's some great marketing and social media lessons to be learned here:

1. **Be creative and innovative.** This product line has gone beyond just a clever hat to include fashionably innovative scarves for women, reversible beanies, hats for toddlers, bendable mos for Movember, bottle-top stashes, and

custom beard colour combos. The company markets to the southern hemisphere's winter during Canadian summers. They're a year-round business by virtue of having global reach and an Internet-based virtual store. Smart.

2. **Have a product that invites talk.** Quirky photos, irreverent video. This is a feel-good and fun product. It's a perfect distraction to send a friend when they should be preparing for a meeting. YouTube views 1.3 million and counting: http://www.youtube.com/watch?v=Nwt6OrQHj6Q. I dare you *not* to watch it!

3. **Fuel the story initially using social.** Instagram, Pintrest, and YouTube were perfect platforms for this very visual product. Facebook and Twitter further gained organic word of mouse and mobile.

4. **Work social media to earn the interest of traditional media.** Then repurpose national and international TV, radio, and print on social to gain further recognition. Wash, rinse, and repeat.

5. **Have a plan for when imitators come to market.** While I'm sure Jeff secured a patent on his design, low-price imitators are bound to come calling. On this point, I am not sure where the young company stands, other than to say the cult-like following of their target segment likely values authenticity as part of the story of ownership. Provided Beardo can continue to cultivate their story and be innovative, they can likely sustain the ride.

Sam Sung, a Specialist for Apple?

• • •

This piece originally appeared in October 2012. I've added an update at the end.

Shortly after this card was posted online about a day ago, **Twitter** and **Facebook** went crazy sharing it. And for good reason. Could there be anything more entertaining than imagining that Sam Sung '**Samsung**' is actually working for **Apple**? Or perhaps considered the other way, the possibility that Apple would hire Sam Sung as a specialist for their products.

Photo: Mary Charleson. Photographed and reproduced with permission by Sam Sung

When I first saw this card, it was framed as likely being a hoax, albeit a clever one to perhaps fuel an online viral marketing campaign.

But if you know anything about printing, you will understand that the reflection on the Apple logo indicates a foil application—a rather expensive one-off endeavour for someone to make this card up. That and the fact that, being from Vancouver and an Apple customer at this store, I knew the address, phone, and website to be accurate.

I visited the Apple store this afternoon and was able to verify that yes, indeed, Sam Sung works there. In fact he has since 2010. Apple staff were however rather guarded around my enquiry, acknowledging that the card had gone viral very quickly. And it appears that a previous LinkedIn profile for Sam Sung in Vancouver has now been removed. Curious . . .

That fact that Sam Sung, as shown in his **LinkedIn** profile prior to its removal, is a marketing graduate intrigues me.

Could this be the cleverest personal branding viral campaign ever? Might Sam Sung be able to leverage it for his own personal gain? You betcha!

Since this article first appeared, I had the occasion to actually be helped by Sam Sung at Apple recently. Initially I just thought the product specialist I was dealing with was exceedingly knowledgeable and helpful. And I had found myself musing at the unusual contradiction of his thick Scottish accent with obvious Chinese heritage. But it was only when I asked for his card to note some product details that I realized who I was dealing with. Once noted, I relayed to him how his card had gone viral several months back and how I had written about it in *Business in Vancouver.* He was gracious, perhaps a little embarrassed, and exceedingly professional. Yes, indeed Sam Sung does work for Apple. And he is good!

What Is Your Brand?

. . .

Hello, my name is Scott. Well, not really, but that's what **Scott Ginsberg** would say upon making your acquaintance. Scott has made a name for himself by wearing a name tag literally every day for the last five years. Initially it was a social experiment by a somewhat socially awkward, but fearlessly challenging youth. Then it became a social network, a type of analogue friend request as strangers introduced themselves and conversations were struck. Then it became permission to market himself and his ideas. It evolved into his statement. Now it has made him memorable. In fact, so memorable he has permanently tattooed it on his chest. Scott is Scott's brand.

His take on all this? 'If you don't make a name for yourself, someone else will.' He further challenges, 'What do people think when they hear your name? What are you known for? What do you stand for?'

What is your brand? Wow. There's a question to ponder.

That's exactly the question I asked a group of students who gathered for the **MiniEnterprize Youth Entrepreneurship Conference**, hosted by **UBC's Sauder School of Business** (http://www.minienterprize.org/).

While I spoke on marketing, specifically, **'5-Minute Marketing—Savvy Advice for Small Business in an Accelerated World'**, at the heart were questions around business and personal branding and identity.

There is much talk about the inability of youth to 'launch' and gain meaningful careers, often saddled with debt and poor job entry prospects these days. Much has been written recently of our antiquated post-secondary education systems, slow to adapt, that aren't educating leaders of tomorrow, but rather cultivating debt for today. I believe this is an incredibly rich time of opportunity for those motivated to either launch their own business or those who recognize the power of personal branding. Never before has there been a generation with so much online influence and potential to build a personal brand. Whether you want to market a business, market your ideas, or market yourself, you need to understand branding and promotion.

I'm not suggesting that we all need to go out and wear a name tag. That's been done. Check out more on Scott here: http://www. hellomynameisscott.com/. I am however suggesting that personal branding, identity, and creative promotion is the marketing edge to separate you from the pack.

Find Your Niche and Do What You Love—Marketing Advice to Treasure

■ ■ ■

Think back to your childhood and the utter delight of imagining buried treasure. Treasures have a story and a historical connection to the past; perhaps that's why their promise holds such intrigue.

Now imagine having a business as a full-time treasure hunter. That's exactly what Chris Turner, **The Ring Finder** (www.theringfinders.com), does. I met Chris at **Grouse Mountain** recently. I was downloading after doing the Grouse Grind, and he was returning from a successful mission to retrieve a visitor's ring in the snow.

I was absolutely fascinated by his story for a couple of reasons:

- **He has a niche business offering**: he is a metal detector detective. He reunites people with their lost items.
- **There is a well-defined target market**: people with sentimental and valuable pieces of jewelry, lost keys, and other items that were thought to have been lost forever.
- **He has differentiated his business and strategy**: he offers retrieval services in the lower mainland, will travel for a fee, or he will link you through his directory to associated providers worldwide.
- **His business grew out of a childhood passion**: at twelve, he saw an ad for a metal detector in his dad's magazine, saved up, and bought one. He's been hooked ever since.

- **He loves what he does and ultimately makes people happy**: he's in the smile business.
- **He works on a reward basis**: customers pay what they think his service is worth and what they can afford. He's worked for a $1,000 and he's worked for a loaf of banana bread.
- **He donates 15% of revenue to Children's Hospital**: giving back is priceless.

He used to get four calls a year and now gets more than seventy-five, mostly due to referrals, networking, and online search. I asked him what was the most common retrieval in eighteen years of business. 'Wedding rings. Taken off and thrown in the heat of an argument with immediate regret. I've had many of those!' notes Chris. And the most memorable story? 'Well, that would have to be the couple from Australia. They were traveling through the Rockies by car. She had taken off five rings, gifts from her late husband, and rolled them in the fold of her shirt while putting on hand lotion. She completely forgot about them when they got out at the roadside to take a photo. It wasn't until they were about to board their flight back to Australia from Calgary that she realized what had happened. She was devastated. They boarded the plane, but the fellow returned several months later, rented a car, and found the roadside spot based solely on the photo he had taken there. With a fork, forging in the dirt on two separate days, he retrieved two rings. He returned to Australia, but a year later, he came back, this time employing my services to find the other three rings. We drove the stretch from Calgary to a GPS setting he had taken. We passed miles and miles of roadside construction, and I could literally feel his heart sink. Remarkably as we rounded the corner to the spot where they had been lost, the crew was still short of the site. With my metal detector, we were able to find the remaining three rings. It was a remarkable story.'

Of course Chris is a boy with his toys. Packing a bag full of super sleuth stuff, he looked to be a cross between a pirate and James Bond. He's now planning to launch a service to exclusive resorts for the über rich. He figures they lose things too, and they are likely to pay handsomely for retrieval. That and the fact that the resorts accepting their $50,000-100,000+ per-night stay on exclusive islands would be equally motivated to satisfy their guests. And there just might be exotic travel involved.

What's the marketing lesson in this story? Have a distinct business offering that's valued by your target audience and not easily copied. Know your target segment, and cater your product/ service offering, pricing, promotion, and distribution with that target in mind. And finally, do what you love. If you take care of everything else, profit will follow.

Making a Business Case
for Social Media

. . .

Much has been written about the power of social media to connect people and to potentially connect people to your product. Beyond the fun stuff and personal use, there is real value for businesses using these tools, but many owners echo the refrain that they want to see an ROI and an improvement to the bottom line. Is that the best way to measure the value of social media? I would argue not.

Although the bottom line is ultimately what business is striving to improve, there are at least three good reasons apart from sales for using social media: to gain market insights, to increase brand or business visibility, and to increase customer loyalty.

1. **Gain market insights:** I rank market research as one of the most critical benefits. Business owners can pay a lot of money for research and insight on their brand. However, courtesy of the web and social media, often many of those insights are available for the taking. You just have to know where to look, be tapped in, and be monitoring activity actively. Add in the benefit of timeliness and truthfulness, and it starts to look like not a bad anecdotal qualitative research tool. Learning what your customers think about your brand, products, or services through the unfiltered and unfretted social media consumer window is priceless. In a recent Marketer's benchmark survey conducted by Focus.com, 49% of business to consumer brands cited improving client understanding as the highest strategic

priority for 2011. Social media will be at the heart of those efforts.

2. **Increase visibility:** Brand or business visibility can be increased substantially using social media. Social media has a bearing on search. Most search engines use a form of blended search, which means they don't just pull from traditional websites, but from various media—YouTube, blogs, Twitter, Facebook, LinkedIn, Foursquare, Gowalla, Flickr, Yelp. If you don't have a presence on some form of social media, you will have less ubiquity. Neilson Media reports that 70% of consumers trust consumer opinions posted online and that 90% of major purchases are researched online prior to purchase. How you show up on your website is important, but increasingly important is what others now say about you online.

3. **Improve customer loyalty:** The customer loyalty loop is increasingly important, not only for its role in influencing the initial purchase, but also that customers' role in potentially influencing other customers in the future. A loyal customer online using social media can be a friend indeed. And as consumers increasingly turn to the web for research on brands before buying, that existing loyal customer is actually an extension of your sales and marketing force. Social media fosters the building of community around the brand. Fans and those they influence don't require nearly the intensity of sales focus that less-engaged prospects do. Again, the Marketer's benchmark survey revealed that 49% of business to consumer brands planned to improve brand awareness, and 40% planned to improve customer retention in 2011 using social media.

To me it seems obvious that these three factors do ultimately effect the bottom line, albeit indirectly, and that has been the challenge in justifying investment of both money and time for many small businesses.

Here is a great resource for businesses wanting to get up to speed on this topic: www.socialquickstarter.com. This site is geared to both those getting started and more sophisticated users, guiding you with both video and written content on areas such as an introduction to social media, Facebook, LinkedIn, blogging, YouTube, ratings and reviews tools, location-based services, QR codes, and e-mail marketing with social media. It's a great one-stop shop and how-to guide in helping you understand and use social media to your advantage.

Winning Over Purchasers
with a Purse

■ ■ ■

Like many lower mainlanders, I found myself one November in a panic to buy snow tires. I've known for close to a year that I needed to buy a new set, but there's nothing like a few flakes falling from the sky to turn casual interest into buying mode. I had done my research online, consulted my panel of experts, phoned around for scheduling availability, and remarkably had ended up at my dealer. After recovering from a $1,300 quote for tires and rims, I learned it that didn't include tire caps. At $100 apiece, they would have put the deal well over $1,700. However, it was assumption that I didn't want them that set me back. I think the conversation went something like this:

Service Guy: 'Well, they're expensive, and you don't really need them. Your car is going to be dirty in the winter anyway. I wouldn't worry about it.'

Me: 'So after spending $1,300, I get to drive a car around that looks like crap?'

Service Guy: 'Oh, you're one of those.'

Not sure what 'one of those' puts me in the company of, but it didn't sound good. However, judging by the reaction of women I relay the story to, most of them shared the same thought. Aesthetics are important. If you believe a vehicle is an extension of who you are, the care you take, and what you value, the tire caps matter—even if it is a minivan! *While function is important, women will always consider the design in the context of function.*

Further driving this lesson home was an outing to replace the rechargeable battery on a video camera. My previous battery was small and light. I was told that I could get a battery that would hold a far longer charged for half the cost. I initially thought that the extra size and weight was an issue, but I succumbed to the salesman's persuasive argument about increased function and cost savings. To this day, I curse the extra size and weight and regret not sticking to my intuitive and more expensive tastes to buy the smaller battery. *In both the tire and battery cases, I was an easy up sell to spend more by recognizing the importance of aesthetics and ease of use, which are both important for women.*

One of my girlfriends recently remarked at the archaic state of paint can design. Lamenting that skinny little wire to carry a heavy can and the inevitable drips down the side of the tin and the gummy top that would never seal properly again, she wondered why paint cans haven't been improved. I told her about Dutch Boy's twist-and-pour cans, complete with a side handle, drip-catching moat, and tool-free twist cap that had won one of them a best package design award and had tripled their sales in six months after introduction. She wondered why it hadn't caught on. Good question, considering the buying power of women making paint choices. *She of course was considering the entire experience of carrying the can and applying the paint, not just the final result, which is reflective of women's holistic approach to purchase decisions.*

Giddy with excitement, a friend declared over drinks recently that she had bought 'hot pants' through a Groupon offer. These hot pants were in fact *hot* pants, which promised to heat up the midsection and cause weight loss. Once we all recovered from the laughter of her plans to wear them while lying in bed watching TV and eating licorice, we enquired about the advertising details behind the promo. It obviously had to be good, since apparently 100s of other Vancouverites had signed up to have them shipped from England. After she recounted the endorsements, relatively low cost, and promise of quick results, we agreed she had not only bought hot pants, she had bought hope.

A summary of these random consumer encounters reveals some lessons: *Women care about aesthetics. Both form and function matter. They are critical of good design. And they buy hope.* Considering she makes or influences 80% of purchases, these are worth noting.

What Apple Has Taught Us About Great Marketing

■ ■ ■

Steve is gone, in what seemed mere weeks after leaving the top job at Apple, the company he founded. The bitter irony that millions would learn of his death via a device he invented was not lost on us. Over the course of his tenure, Steve Jobs led Apple on a wild ride and changed our world irrevocably. Arguably he was one of the best marketers out there. Here's why:

He understood product innovation and design. By my count, he introduced five disruptive technologies.

1. He invented the personal computer. Emphasis on *personal*. It was nothing like the hulking mainframes sitting in airtight controlled rooms that were being introduced at the time to house and crunch data.
2. He gave us Apples and Macs specifically. He told us a mouse wasn't a rodent, but rather an intuitive device to navigate a desktop. He made it possible to print a document by pointing to something that looked like a printer in a pull-down menu, and not some geeky series of key commands. I remember being a CS100 student at the University of Waterloo in 1984 and being the study group for thirty new Apple Macs. The ease of use to a non-computer-science student was driven home in a subsequent work term at IBM prior to Windows' launching. What a difference!
3. He changed the music industry forever with the iPod and had the foresight to understand that the distribution

system for digitized content was key to the success of that product, so he invented iTunes.

4. The iPhone changed the way we communicate and access the web on the go. Suddenly to call it a phone was a humble misrepresentation, when it also had become a camera, a computer, a music player, a TV, a GPS navigation system, an e-mail platform, a voice recorder, and had endless other capabilities through apps. He didn't invent the one-million-plus apps out there, but he made it so others could.

5. He has shown us that the iPad will be the most disruptive technology the computing industry has seen. It is challenging the desktop and laptop categories. And it will change the distribution of print and broadcast media, as well as book industries just like the iPod changed the music industry.

In each of these five major launches, Steve Jobs had the uncanny ability to give us something we wanted before we knew we needed it. While other companies change, copy, and upgrade products, few have invented with such success. He not only strategically saw an opportunity and evolution of the effected industries before he entered them; he moulded them to his liking along the way.

He understood the principles of good design. Apple products are intuitive, simple, and sexy.

He understood the impact of great advertising. Good design plus good advertising makes for a lustful combination. Few have created so many products that customers (shall we say, fans?) lust over.

He understood the importance of the distribution system as a marketing tool. He created iTunes to integrate with iPod and disrupted the music industry forever. He created Apple stores to ensure a consistent retail experience. He didn't go for mass distribution; he went for strategic retail representation in keeping with the premium pricing strategy.

He understood the importance of showmanship and sales. Apple, the king of 'controlled leaks', knows how to create anticipation around product launches like few other companies. It doesn't hurt that many of your customers are already rabid fans.

And it now looks like Apple has set its sights on disrupting the TV industry and distribution channels for content. That will be one to watch as the line between computers and TV disappears.

In short, Steve Jobs was a visionary and a great marketer. His footprint has irrevocably changed our society for the better.

The Web Grows Up

■ ■ ■

Web 1.0 could be summed up as 'brochures online'. Businesses raced to put online what they had in print. Early sites featured home-made design and cookie-cutter graphics. Thankfully we moved on quickly from there and handed the process over to designers. Dinosaur alert if you still belong to this first category.

Web 2.0 emerged a number of years ago. This phase featured two-way exchanges and interactivity on websites, blogs, and social media. Content was refreshed, new material added, and conversations were engaged. Viral became king, and the consumer had a voice.

We have now entered the early stages of Web 3.0. This phase was signaled by shifts in three pivotal areas: measuring, monitoring, and monetization.

1. Measuring the right thing.

Remember when measuring the web was all about impressions and hits? While these are still important, measuring *the right thing* is more important. The 450 million views of the Subservient Chicken video for **Burger King** generated lots of online viral buzz. However, a year later, sales were actually down, sending their stock price sliding 20%. The average viewer spent six minutes, which is a huge time for engagement. But were they measuring the right thing? As we emerge into Web 3.0, we will measure more than just viral views, time of engagement, and social media mentions. We will want to know how it delivers sales.

2. Monitoring is key.

New systems are emerging to monitor social media mentions, the digital crumb trail of consumers, where, when, and how engagement occurred and on what platform. However, in the end, the only monitor that will matter is the objective of the advertiser and the ability of the campaign to deliver. In the hard-fought cola wars, **Pepsi** recently fell to third behind **Coke** and **Diet Coke**. Why? Industry observers have suggested that Pepsi's decision to drop the reach of traditional TV media in favour of online may have provoked the situation. Coke invested in TV, the Super Bowl, and sponsorship. The lesson here seems to be integrated marketing communications is key. Online on its own is not the magic bullet. In fact, in isolation, it can hurt the cause.

3. Monetization of web content.

While the purchase of goods and services on the web has been largely accepted, monetizing the value of information has struggled. The *New York Times* recently instituted a user pay wall. Essentially non-subscribers will be limited to five Google search links per day prior to being asked to pay. Curiously views linked from Facebook and Twitter will be unlimited and free. This was likely done for two reasons: (1) to fuel viral social sharing of content; and (2) to keep the most vocal and web-savvy online crowd happy.

The iPad users can now subscribe online to their favourite magazines and newspapers. Apple takes 30% of the subscription fee, but more importantly owns the subscriber information. This has bristled some publishers and is likely to lead to Apple's control of the ad delivery platform with targeted user data. Apple is doing to print media with the iPad what it did to music with the iPod.

What are the implications of all this? Monetization will change the model of content delivery and how companies that produce that content will make money. This shift is profound. It will create new media moguls and dwarf former titans. During the web 2.0

phase, we became almost convinced that giving content away for free was okay because everyone else was doing it. As with any market correction, we are now realizing that all things free are not necessarily equal. The web has grown up. It's time to use tools that work in the boardroom—that means measuring, monitoring, and monetizing.

Ready, Aim, Fire!

■ ■ ■

Ready. Aim. Fire! It's a sequence of actions familiar to anyone trying to hit a target. Be it for the purpose of scoring on an opponent or eliminating a pesky wasp nest, execute it in the wrong order, and you'll fail to achieve your goal, or worse, get stung!

Then why is it that many businesses mess up their marketing by getting the order wrong, or even missing one of the steps? They fire off in all directions with the latest 'got to have' tools in their marketing arsenal. They've got to be on Facebook and LinkedIn. They're tweeting stuff and following others. They're creating YouTube channels and posting video. They're blogging, sending e-newsletters, and building an e-mail database and tracking website traffic. They're playing with location-based mobile applications. Heck, they might even be creating their own app, because as everyone knows, apps and mobile media are the future of marketing.

What's wrong with all this? Nothing provided the preparation work of *ready* and *aim* has precluded it. I am a huge advocate of e-marketing, social media, and mobile applications in particular. These are great tools, provided they're used with focus and preparation. But if you *fire* before you're ready, and if you don't *aim* at a target, aim at too many, or choose the wrong one, the results are bound to be less than what they could have been.

Let's take a look at each area:

Ready:
Although most people assume they're ready, there are some big-picture questions to ask. What am I selling? What is our expertise?

Who will buy it? How am I positioned in the marketplace compared to my competitors? What is my distinct competency? What is it that I do better than anyone else that is desirable to the marketplace and is not easily copied?

Aim:
Once you're ready, then it's time to take aim with your marketing. Your marketing needs to reflect the benefits of dealing with your business and what makes your brand different and special. You might ask the following questions. What is the essence of my brand? How are we different? What is my brand promise? What are the outcomes of dealing with my business? The goal is for your target customer group to say, 'Yes, we need that!' And just who is your target audience? Define your perfect customer. You need to go beyond a demographic and geographic definition here, to define how they think, act, and feel as well as what they value. The more specific the characteristics, the better, since these will help you determine how best to reach the audience in the *fire* phase when you finally reach out to your market.

Fire:
This is where you get to be both creative in your execution and media choices. But the key is to tightly correlate the behaviours of the group you defined in the *aim* phase with the techniques you choose to reach out. You may use traditional media, new social and mobile media, or a combination of the two. Or you might use direct selling techniques. It really depends on who your perfect customer is and how you are best to permeate their world.

The key point here is this: do not fire before you are ready and have taken aim. It confuses the marketplace, and frankly, it can be a waste of money, time, and effort. In a media world with lots of new toys and tools at our disposal, it is tempting to *fire* off in all directions trying stuff out. But the same marketing rules still apply. Do your preparation work first!

Brand Canada

■ ■ ■

Do you remember a scene from the Tourism Canada commercial during the 2010 Winter Olympics where a young hockey player skates across an untouched frozen lake at sunset? Viewed from above, his pace quickens as the endless lake beckons. It's an image that those of us raised outside the lower mainland may have experienced once or twice in a lifetime, when the perfect alignment of a big freeze and no snow early in the season offers up the quintessential Canadian experience. This memorable piece of footage, captured by a helicopter film crew over Green Lake, was an unplanned ending to a day filming in Whistler to capture 2010 image resources for media. According to **John Parker-Jervis, senior media advisor, Canadian Tourism Commission,** the film crew spotted the scrimmage on the lake and landed to get permission to capture it. The resulting breakaway hockey player became one of the iconic images that captured and embodied the 'experience Canada' brand. It was a brilliant piece of luck. But there was a strategy behind it.

Now that our streets, then filled with patriotism and hockey gold, have returned to normal, we can pause to consider: Was there more to marketing Canada through the games than a two-week-long commercial? Absolutely, but let's admit with some smugness that the ten days of sun and warm weather in February broadcast worldwide to 3.5 billion people certainly didn't hurt.

These were called Canada's games, and viewed from a marketing perspective, they were one of the most successful branding exercises I have witnessed in some time. Canada the brand, defined by experiences, became hip and desirable. No longer are we just selling moose, mountains, and Mounties.

So how was the Olympics used to reposition Canada the brand and strategically target international tourism markets? Environics, a Toronto-based firm known for social values research, had identified nine basic traveler groups worldwide. Having a detailed demographic, psychographic, and values-based profile for each, Canada was then positioned to appeal to three categories: the *authentic experiencer*, the *cultural explorer*, and the *free spirit*. Specific countries with a high proportion of these groups were identified as strategic targets for a before-, during-, and after-Olympic campaign strategy.

Before:
Fifteen spots were secured in the cross-Canada torch relay for past Olympic medalists and media celebrities from targeted tourism countries, including Korea, Japan, China, India, Australia, Brazil, Germany, France, the UK, and the US. Torchbearers spent time in the areas they were running and enjoyed local tourism experiences. Many areas across Canada were represented. Home country media covered these celebrities extensively. In the summer of 2009, selected 2010 international athletes with their families were brought to Canada to experience unique adventures through the 'Connecting with Canadians program'. Video footage of their travels at specific targeted tourism destinations throughout Canada was shared with media in international markets. The goal was to make the winter games resonate with targeted countries by making it relevant and to plant a desire to explore Canada in the future. One NBC feature about travel experiences in the north's polar bear country actually resulted in overloaded website traffic for the tour operator featured due to subsequent enquiries from Americans.

During:
The Canadian Tourism Commission made available extensive resources for the media, including travel story ideas, high-definition video clips and still images of Canadian travel

destinations, athletes, torchbearers, as well as venue and host city aerials. These were all easily accessible and rights free. Provincial pavilions represented travel destinations throughout Canada during the games. The Northern pavilion alone had over 250,000 visitors. Meeting planners from around the world were hosted and extensive work was done with First Nations groups to present unique experiences of their culture.

After:
Now it's all about harvesting the afterglow. Efforts now focus on ensuring a smooth continuum from awareness and interest to planning and booking. Already there have been huge jumps in website visits from Japan, Korea, and China, as well as Germany, the UK, and the US. Social media is being leveraged extensively during this phase. The updraft in bookings is expected during 2011 and 2012 from the interest created.

As Shane Koyczan, the slam poet who delivered the 'Define Canada' piece during the opening ceremonies, put it, 'We are an experiment going right for a change.' That experiment packaged in unique experiences now defines brand Canada.

M UTH
M USE &
M BILE

CHAPTER 4

Advertising Creativity

. . .

One of the refreshing things I enjoy about working in marketing is having a venue for personal creativity as well as being around truly creative people. They're the ones that see a different angle for an image, coin a phrase just the right way to give multiple meaning, instinctively understand how to connect brands with stories, and see potential media vehicles are around us. This chapter looks at creative executions, rooted in storytelling to leverage word of mouth, mouse, and mobile.

129

Dove Real Beauty Sketches

• • •

I love this new campaign by Dove.

Photo: Used with permission by Fernando Machado, Unilever

It features a forensic sketch artist creating images of women as they describe themselves and as others, who they have recently met, see them. All images where created without actually seeing the person, instead relying on how each person interview described them. Subjects were then shown the images created side by side and asked to ponder the differences and perhaps how their personal view is distorted. As a group of women, the outcomes are all similar—the images created as others saw them were always more attractive than as they saw themselves. You can view the three-minute video here: http://www.youtube.com/watch?v=XpaOjMXyJGk.

I interviewed Janet Krestin, at the time, the creative director at Ogilvy Toronto, shortly after Dove embarked on this approach with the 'Campaign for Real Beauty' back in 2004. At the time, she referred to it as a movement that would likely take twenty years and a generation to impact change rather than a campaign. Although it sounded good, I had my doubts that any agency or client could sustain the same approach through various creative reiterations, little lone changes in staff, possible agency switches, etc. I have to say that this is a completely fresh look at the same theme. They're almost at year 10. Quite something.

I received a link to this video from a female friend, who had shared it with a large group of women. She wasn't pushing product or advocating for a particular company. She was simply sharing something that she thought creative, interesting, and worthy of our time. And that was exactly the goal of the campaign. Judging from the 55.2 million views to date on YouTube, I'd say she was one of many.

In the end, on some level it's about gaining market share and commercial interests. But on an altruistic level, which I think they can take ownership of with some authenticity, I'd like to believe it's about a little bit more.

And just in case you need a little contrasting view mixed with humour, the parodies to this spot have already hit YouTube. Check out the male version of this spot. And yes, you guessed it, the guys are far less critical of themselves. In fact, they're quite the opposite (https://www.youtube.com/watch?feature=player_embedded&v=T8Jiwo3u6Vo)!

Clever Creative: One Ad, Two Targets, and Two Messages

■ ■ ■

This came to me via one of my students, and I thought it worthy of sharing with a larger audience—primarily for the creative approach to segmentation, but also for its message. This work comes out of Spain and was done for the ANAR Foundation (Aid to Children and Adolescents at Risk Foundation). In an effort to provide abused children a safe way to reach out for help, the ad actually shows a different visual as well as written message to children compared to adults based on their height and viewing angle. While adults view an image of a child with the message 'Sometimes child abuse is only visible to the child suffering it', children from a lower viewing angle see the same child with a bruised cheek and cut lip and the message 'If somebody hurts you, phone us and we'll help you', along with a phone number displayed. It of course assumes that children under ten can read the message and are empowered to make the cell phone call, which is perhaps a stretch for some, and it also assumes the kids understand that the adults cannot see the message that they see. It's particularly powerful if their abuser happens to be standing right next to them.

ANAR Foundation Campaign, used with permission.
Creative by Grey, Spain

The very presence or need for this type of ad is disturbing, but it does highlight a very creative approach to segmentation and messaging put to work for a good purpose. What might be the possible dark side? Toy companies or fast-food restaurants taking this approach to coax children into wanting something with a hidden message that their parents can't see. Hmmmm . . .

Watch a video about the billboard here and see how it works: https://www.youtube.com/watch?v=6zoCDyQSH0o

Creativity in the Streets: Get Noticed and Get Business

■ ■ ■

Turning everyday objects into ads can be a clever vehicle to leverage a campaign. As many of you know, the coffee wars between McDonald's, Tim Hortons, and Starbucks have heated up significantly in Canada. While it may seem no accident that McDonald's executes a major push, with week long free coffee giveaways which over-lapped several times with Tim Hortons' Roll Up the Rim to Win campaigns, the company has been actively growing presence and market share with their McCafé coffee campaigns and promotions that run several times a year. This April 2009 cheeky street ad appeared as part of a free coffee give away promotion to get McDonald's coffee into the hands of consumers. Now that's pretty hard to ignore!

Used with permission from McDonald's Corporation. Creative by Cossette West.
Photo: Alastair Bird with permission.

Here's another interesting one, courtesy of an effort to clean up the Milwaukee River by driving people to a website to donate. Again, the juxtaposition of objects being used out of context pushes the creative to be noticed.

Photo: Scott Ritenour. Used with permission by STIR, Milwaukee

And here's one from downtown Vancouver. Art Stafford is in the tax preparation business, and he borrowed this idea from an application his son saw in Britain.

Photo: Mary Charleson

He's found a clever way to get around street sign bi-laws that would normally prohibit such signs being attached to poles. Mounted to the back of a bike, which is then chained to the pole, it becomes a free ad complete with takeaway business cards. Art has been putting the bike ad out for the last five years, during three months leading up to tax time. He claims to get about 100 clients per year from the stunt.

Bottom line? Creativity = business!

Place and Purpose Creativity Winners and Losers

. . .

Sometimes creativity just requires a slightly different perspective on things. Take this bus shelter ad for example. Displayed upright, it would be just like any other. Made into a ramp, it takes on purpose and meaning to a target group of skateboarders.

Photo: Quicksilver image used with permission by Simon Wooler, Saatchi & Saatchi, Copenhagen

However, this misplaced Turkish Airlines ad is quite comical. What on earth were they thinking?

Image source: www.flight.org, Feb 6, 2010

To be fair, I was informed that this Turkish Airlines banner was erected in error. The flip side of the escalator has the same image in reverse—so the aircraft is climbing rather than crashing. The image was apparently taken down after two days. Still, it's the kind of thing that makes you scratch your head—didn't the person putting this up think about what they were actually doing?

Place and purpose can make or break creative. Just be sure to use it wisely. Likewise, consideration of location and your target group, and yes, orientation of that creative!

Biggest Social Media Disasters of 2012

. . .

Like an accident scene, it seems we can't resist the temptation to stop and crane our necks and gaze at others' misfortune. This year's biggest social media disasters can be best summed up in three categories:

1. **Insensitive: The Gap** and **American Apparel** take the prize here. Both retailers got caught encouraging consumers on Twitter to shop or take advantage of special discounts during Hurricane Sandy. That they appeared to be exploiting the fact that many were off work with time on their hands is quite shallow. Good on Twitter followers for calling them out on it.
2. **Bad timing:** The **NRA (National Rifle Association)** takes the award here. While it appears to have been a pre-scheduled tweet on Hootsuite, they found themselves encouraging members to have shooting plans, it being Friday and the end of the week. Trouble was, right when the tweet was going out was the exact same time that the mass theatre shooting was taking place in Aurora, Colorado. Ouch.

   Equally poorly timed was **Kitchen Aid's** suggestion that even Obama's grandmother knew the election results would be bad, since she died three days before the results were in. This was not only bad timing, and insensitive, but also flat-out stupid political game playing.

3. **Customers turning on you:** While this is not the first time customers have turned on a company trying to leverage gain through promoted tweets, both **McDonald's** and **Snickers** learned the hard way that a campaign planned to promote their brands could actually have the exact opposite effect. Have we learned nothing about the consumer owning your message, folks? Unbelievable for two brands that should have known better.

For a close-up personal look, check out this link: http://on.mash.to/TeXdxt. I've only highlighted six. There are four more that made the top ten!

Election Protection— JetBlue Scores a Marketing Campaign Winner

■ ■ ■

South of the border when things were heating up with the US presidential election, election campaigns were usually full of promises—lower taxes, better healthcare, more jobs. But what if someone promised you a free flight to leave the country if your chosen candidate didn't win? That's exactly what **JetBlue** did with their November marketing campaign '**2012 Election Protection— Live Free or Fly**'.

Fearing the country would immediately go to the dogs if their candidate loses, those who respond to the contest had a chance to leave on a free flight. All they had to do is visit the airline's website and register their vote. There were 1,006 tickets given away to a possible twenty-one destinations. The company also encouraged Americans to get out and vote.

This was a cheeky and clever marketing campaign aimed at garnering publicity far beyond the purchased buy. It was fun, it cut through the clutter, and it milked a timely event—all golden rules for getting publicity. It was also a great way to capture customer information and to leverage it in future campaigns. Arguably, knowing which side of the political battle Americans align with would also enable the company to position with humour, segmented marketing communications.

Check out the campaign here:
http://www.jetblueelectionprotection.com/.

Could we ever see something this clever in Canada? Well, first we'd have to have a political run-off worth the excitement, which appears at best distant. With the exception of Justin Trudeau's recently launched run at leadership for the beleaguered third-place Liberal party of Canada, we've been stripped of anything with charismatic appeal on the political stage. Perhaps that's why we watch with envy the battle south of the border. Trudeau may well pull a page from the late Jack Layton's playbook and position himself as the cute, charismatic, and capable Justin, rather than running on the divisive yet famous name of his father and long-time Prime Minister Pierre Trudeau. And the only airline that has a cheeky-enough personality to mimic the 'Don't like it, leave' approach of JetBlue would be WestJet. But until then, kudos to JetBlue for their timely creativity. Well done.

Social Media and Public Relations Lessons 'Out of the Blue'

■ ■ ■

Some brands sign celebrities for endorsement of their products. Strategically selected for their alignment with brand values and appeal to the brand target group, it's a formal arrangement offering financial gain for both parties.

What then to do when a self-appointed celebrity selects your brand and you unwittingly become dragged into a negative association not of your own making? That's exactly what happened with Labatt in June 2012, when a photo of the now-infamous Canuck cannibal killer Luka Magnotta surfaced, courtesy of the *Montreal Gazette*, holding a tin of Labatt's Blue. While the paper could be accused of inflaming the story for their own readership gain, having selected the photo from hundreds available on Magnotta's Facebook page, it was the actions of Labatt's lawyers that drew the attention that ultimately turned the story into a public relations nightmare.

Simply put, the lawyers acted in a command control manner, as though they could reprimand the *Gazette* in a vacuum. Of course the world of social media would have none of that, and it wasn't long before someone on Facebook speculated it was all a cleverly shielded campaign by Labatt to gain attention. Before long, someone else had created a hashtag on Twitter #newlabattcampaign. That's when, in the words of Malcolm Gladwell, 'it tipped'. News of the supposed campaign spread and actually became a trending topic on Twitter in Canada the following week. Clever yet tasteless headlines, such as 'I would give an arm and a leg for a Labatt Blue' and 'Labatt Blue: All beer, no head', were bantered about while the creation of campaign one-liners became sport for many. It only came to a halt when, thankfully, the public relations department rescued the lawyers mired in unfamiliar social media territory. Labatt retracted their threat to sue the *Gazette* and simply stated that they had been trying to protect their brand. An earnest cause for sure, but unfortunately, they learned the hard way that consumers owned the message, not the lawyers in corporate headquarters.

For me what became painfully obvious in all this was the utter importance of having brand equity and good will in the bank, so if need be in times of crisis, some equity can be squandered, while still maintaining brand value. Framed from a different perspective, I'm not sure had Mr. Magnotta been sporting a Molson Canadian would the resulting fallout have been the same. Molson has invested heavily in brand building, aligning themselves closely with brand Canada since the 2010 Winter Olympics. I don't think the social media sphere would have turned so quickly on something that tapped that inner connection to Canadian values.

While Labatt hasn't used their 1998 campaign line, 'A whole lot can happen out of the blue,' for some time, they certainly learned that public relations lessons in the age of social media can happen *out of the blue*!

Reality TV Meets Experiential Marketing with a Social Media Twist

■ ■ ■

I love this recent Air New Zealand campaign called 'Kiwi Skeptics', aimed at getting 'Aussies to cross the ditch', or for the rest of us, enticing Australians to visit New Zealand. Seems despite their proximity, many Aussies just don't feel the love for their southern partner, but the geographic proximity makes them a logical travel destination.

Enter a series of reality TV-style produced segments, each six minutes long, featuring four Australians, selected no doubt for their stereotypes, who get tricked into going to New Zealand. Martin, a true-blue Aussie bloke who thinks he's going to Vegas, is particularly memorable. But so is the hipster who thinks he's going to Berlin, the shopping princess who thinks she's off to Bali, or the sophisticated culture critic who thinks she's going to Europe. A film crew and a cheeky Aussie narrator chronicle their travels as they are exposed to a good time, courtesy of their Kiwi companion, while challenging the previously held notions of their neighbouring country. View the segments here: http://www.youtube.com/watch?v=V32jyVFuHRk&feature=relmfu.

Why does this campaign work, and what can we learn from it?

1. The audience is in on the trick, which draws the viewer in.
2. The Aussie stereotypes are characters the target group can identify with.

3. Although the movies are no doubt highly edited and somewhat scripted, they appear like reality TV.
4. The content is entertaining and highly shareable in social media.
5. It has great publicity value, further increasing free coverage through traditional media channels as well as online.

I look forward to watching how this campaign will play out over other media platforms, and in particular, how it will no doubt boost sales for Air New Zealand. Nicely done!

Remote Control Banner Ads? Clever Innovation in Experiential Product Marketing

■ ■ ■

Japanese toy manufacturer Beacon came up with a very creative interactive banner campaign for their toy AR.Drone. While I'm usually reluctant to welcome the possibility of yet another remote-control device in the hands of a male member of my household, this is very intriguing from a marketing perspective!

The AR.Drone is a helicopter that allows owners to use their iPhone as the remote control. To simulate the experience, and to help drive sales, they came up with a banner ad containing a QR code. When viewers scan the QR code on their computer with their iPhone, they get a hook-up that syncs the computer with the iPhone. The iPhone then becomes a remote control for the toy displayed in the banner, essentially bringing it to life. The helicopter can then be flown around the site, dropping bombs and blasting things. While this feature is more apt to appeal to my son or husband, that is absolutely the point. It presents an intriguing way to engage the target market by making the ad into an actual product experience. In linking the devices, users grant the company access to send them additional information and offers. Beacon claims to have had three times the click through for the campaign compared to standard web banners.

Watch the video to see how it works here: http://www.youtube.com/watch?v=88aWyz3Gijk.

Beyond toys, I can certainly see broader applications for this. Audience engagement and involvement has always been key to advertising success. This example helps push those limits a little further!

Is It Time to Disrupt
Your Industry?

. . .

Nobody enjoys a disruption, but it's a fact of life. Kids ask to be picked up in the middle of a great movie. Meetings are scheduled right when you're actually being productive. And occasionally, competitors or a new technology turn an industry on its ear.

Increasingly competition is coming from outside your industry, or influenced by technology that changes your industry. Think of the **iPad** and the publishing industry, or the **iPod** and the music industry.

Grocery shopping is not exactly ripe for innovation. Or is it?

Enter the **Tesco Homeplus virtual subway store** in **South Korea**. They were solidly second as far as awareness and market share in the traditional grocery store model. However, they got creative with a campaign that involved growing their market share and sales without building more stores. They installed large poster images that depicted grocery store isles life-size in subway transit areas. The idea was that viewers could shop by scanning the item with the displayed QR code on their phone and add it to their shopping cart. The items were processed using online payment, and groceries were delivered to their home after they got home. Suddenly wait time had become productive and novel.

In doing this, Homeplus disrupted the traditional distribution channel. No store, no clerks, no inventory. They had a warehouse and delivery trucks at less cost. They disrupted both the pricing model as well as the payment system. Payments were through a mobile wallet. They disrupted the product model. Items were not real, but rather virtual images. There was no spoilage, refrigeration, or restocking. And finally, they disrupted the promotions model. The endeavour attracted media coverage and was a natural for shared social media exposure. Earned media helped spread the word. Plus it was a natural for capturing data user insights for further direct marketing efforts.

What I love about this example is how it not only disrupts one of the legs that strategic marketing is built on (product, price, distribution, promotion), it disrupts all four!

Tesco Homeplus subway store. Creative campaign by Cheil Worldwide, Seoul, South Korea

Watch the **YouTube video** of how they did it at https://www. youtube.com/watch?v=Ups8_f95TOg.

Of course, South Korea had the perfect conditions for this model: A high penetration of smartphone users, availability, awareness, and trust in a mobile wallet service. And they had the right demographic density in urban transit areas to ensure there were enough users to make it a viable endeavour.

With Thanks

. . .

Thank you for adding *Word of Mouth, Mouse, and Mobile* to your library. This book is the result of many years of professional experience as a marketing thought leader, speaker, writer, and strategist. I welcome your questions or comments. E-mail me at mary@charleson.ca.

Join the Conversation or Get Marketing Insights Delivered to Your Inbox

Visit Mary's blog www.fiveminutemarketing.com for fresh weekly insights on marketing topics. Share your thoughts with others through this active community of entrepreneurs, business owners, marketing managers, and students. Or visit Mary's website www.charleson.ca for over ten years of articles and content to help you market your business effectively.

If you enjoyed my book, why not sign up for my regular blog post alerts here: www.fiveminutemarketing.com/subscribe/ And if you'd like to get marketing tips delivered directly to your in box, subscribe to my marketing e-newsletter. Visit www.charleson.ca and select 'Join our mailing list' on the home page.

Bio

. . .

Mary Charleson, MBA, is a marketing educator, speaker, and strategist. She is president of Charleson Communications, a consulting company she established in 1991. Mary's career spans over twenty years in media sales, advertising creative development, production, marketing management, and research. She is the author of *Five-Minute Marketing*, the ultimate marketing how-to guide for the time-starved. Mary delivers keynotes and workshops to help business leaders manage their strategies in an accelerated world. She has taught marketing for City University of Seattle, New York Institute of Technology, UCW, Acsenda School of Management, and Capilano University. She's been entertaining readers of *Business in Vancouver* with her pithy comments and astute observations on marketing trends since 2002. *Marketing Magazine*, *Strategy*, *Marketline*, and the *Toronto Star* have also picked up her writing. For a list of clients and projects, visit www.charleson.ca, or for a sampling of her *5-Minute Marketing* insights, visit her blog at www.fiveminutemarketing.com. Mary is a member of the Canadian Association of Professional Speakers (CAPS) and the voice of 'Five-Minute Marketing' radio podcast. Her first book, *Five-Minute Marketing*, was published in 2010.

Let's Connect

Website:	www.charleson.ca
Blog:	www.fiveminutemarketing.com
Twitter:	https://twitter.com/marycharleson
Google:	https://plus.google.com/u/0/118271779041714550003/about

Facebook Personal:	http://www.facebook.com/maryjcharleson
Facebook Page:	http://www.facebook.com/ fiveminutemarketing
YouTube:	http://www.youtube.com/user/ CharlesonMary?feature=mhum
Book on Amazon:	http://www.amazon.com/Minute-Marketing-Five-minute-articles-marketing/ dp/1426905793/ref=tmm_pap_title_0?ie= UTF8&qid=1372098280&sr=8-1
iTunes podcasts:	https://itunes.apple.com/kw/podcast/5-minute-marketing-mary-charleson/ id477250503

Keynotes, Presentations, and Workshops

■ ■ ■

Canadian Association of Professional Speakers profile:
http://canadianspeakers.org/speaker/5286/

Most Requested Topic: 5-Minute Marketing: Tips, Trends, and Takeaways to Manage in an Accelerated World

Whether you are an entrepreneur or come from a small business or corporate background, Mary makes a complex subject simple. Pithy, often irreverent, but never short on actionable insights, information is presented in a compelling and memorable way—through storytelling, research, and in short 5-minute segments on a variety of marketing topics. After gaining insights on the challenges that a business or industry is facing, Mary selects a series of 5-Minute Marketing insights to meet the client's specific needs, while considering current market trends and opportunities. Tired of other speakers losing your audience after the first 5 minutes? The unique 5-minute segment structure of Mary's approach keeps even the most attention deficit-challenged audiences alert and ready to put insight into action!

Constantly updated with insights from Mary's popular blog (www.fiveminutemarketing.com), this dynamic audio and video rich presentation can stand alone as a keynote, or be used as part of a whole or half day session to lead off a marketing workshop for your company. We'd be happy to discuss your needs and make a recommendation for your meeting, workshop or keynote. Here is a sample of marketing vignettes that can be incorporated into your customized program.

- Tracked, targeted and tired: Consumers go private in public as leading marketing trend. What other trends could affect your industry?
- Social media mistakes: Lessons from top global brands.
- Word of mouth, mouse & mobile: Time to spread the word.
- Social media success stories: Going viral for all the right reasons.
- Branding: Make a name for yourself before someone else does.
- Going mobile: Learn from today's leaders. It's your future!
- Disruption: Learn to love it.
- Path to purchase: It has changed. What to do about it.
- Creative wall of fame & wall of shame: Learning from winners & loosers.
- Is it time to break the rules? Challenge convention and stand out.
- Bought, earned and owned media: Leveraging your publicity.
- Social media: Embrace the consumer that controls your message.